NEW YORK STATE

NAVIGATION

LAW

2019 EDITION

Revised April 23, 2019

By Evgenia Naumchenko

NEW YORK LEGISLATURE

Table of Contents

Article 1 Short Title and Definitions 10
    § 1. Short title 10
    § 2. Definitions 10

Article 2 Administration 14
    § 10. Duties of the commissioner of parks, recreation and historic preservation and the commissioner of environmental conservation 14
    § 11. [Repealed] 14
    § 12. Inspector; qualifications 14
    § 13. Inspector; duties 14
    § 14. Inspector; licenses 15
    § 15. Inspector; fees 15
    § 16. Inspector; reports 15
    § 17. Traveling navigation inspectors 16
    § 18. Special navigation inspectors 16
    § 19. Uniform navigation summons and complaint 16
    § 20. Verification of complaints 18

Article 3 Navigable Waters of the State 18
    § 30. Navigation, jurisdiction over 18
    § 31. Excavation, fill or other modification of water course 19
    § 32. Location of structures in or on navigable waters 19
    § 32-a. Using net or weir unlawfully in Hudson river 20
    § 32-b. Lights upon swing bridges 20
    § 32-c. Interfering with navigation 20
    § 32-d. Dumping or depositing of certain materials in the Genesee river 21
    § 32-e. Restriction and regulation of structures in certain towns and villages in the county of Niagara 21
    § 33. Deposit of refuse in navigable waters of the state 21
    § 33-a. Sanitary facilities aboard craft on Lake George, Canandaigua Lake, Keuka Lake, Skaneateles Lake and on Greenwood Lake, Orange county 22

§ 33-b. Dumping or depositing trash and other debris in Chautauqua lake and its tributaries; ice fishing shanties on lakes within the state of New York; identification of duck blinds..22

§ 33-c. Regulating disposal of sewage; littering of waterways 23

§ 33-d. Sanitary facilities aboard crafts on Lake Champlain 27

§ 33-e. Marine sanitation devices aboard vessels in vessel waste no-discharge zones.............................28

§ 34. Regattas...29

§ 34-a. Permits for racing shell regattas not required 30

§ 35. Aids to navigation..30

§ 35-a. Floating objects other than aids to navigation 31

§ 35-b. Markers for skin or scuba divers 32

§ 35-c. Real time and wind water level telemetry system..32

§ 35-d. Aquatic invasive species signs at public boat launches..33

§ 36. Removal of unauthorized floating object 34

§ 37. Public use of privately owned navigable waters...34

§ 38. Lake George water levels 34

§ 39. Motor boat regulation on Lake George..35

§ 39-a. Motor boat regulation on Lake Colby..36

Article 4 Vessels 37

§ 40. Equipment..37

§ 40-a. Manufacture and sale of outboard motors 40

§ 40-b. Sale and use of tributyltin paint 40

§ 41. Pilot rules...41

§ 42. Searchlights; unlawful to flash 44

§ 42-a. Tow-chains...44

§ 43. Lights to be displayed 45

§ 44. Noise levels on pleasure vessels 48

§ 44-a. [Repealed] 51

§ 44-b. [Repealed] 51

§ 44-c. [Repealed] 51

§ 44-d. [Repealed] 51

§ 44-e. [Repealed] 51

§ 45. Reckless operation of a vessel; speed 51

§ 45-a. Beaching a disabled water craft 53

§ 45-aa. Special provisions relating to reckless operation and speed on Canandaigua lake; Keuka lake 53

§ 45-aaa. Special provisions relating to speed on Irondequoit bay 54

*§ 45-aaaa. Special provisions relating to reckless operation and speed on Greenwood Lake 55

*§ 45-aaaa. Special provisions relating to speed on Sodus Bay 56

§ 45-aaaaa. Special provisions relating to reckless operation and speed on Lake Alice 57

*§ 45-aaaaaa. Special provisions relating to noise and speed on Lamoka Lake and Waneta Lake 57

*§ 45-aaaaaa. Special provisions relating to reckless operation, noise and speed on the Fulton Chain of Lakes 59

§ 45-b. Regulation of beaches 60

§ 45-c. Special provisions relating to reckless operation and speed on Conesus lake 60

§ 45-cc. Reckless operation and speed on the canal system 61

§ 45-d. Special provisions relating to speed at Crooke's Point in Great Kills Harbor 62

§ 46. Vessel regulation zone 62

§ 46-a. Regulations of vessels 64

§ 46-aa. Special provisions relating to speed on lakes in Chautauqua county 67

§ 46-aaa. Special provisions relating to reckless operation and speed on certain lakes in Hamilton county 68

§ 46-aaaa. Special provisions relating to speed on Cuba lake 69

§ 46-b. Special provisions relating to speed on Saratoga lake 70

§ 47. Leaving the scene of an accident without reporting 71

§ 47-a. Accidents; police authorities, bay constables and coroners to report 72

§ 47-b. Report to the commissioner required upon accident 73

§ 48. Negligence in use or operation of vessel attributable to owner 74

§ 49. Operator 77

§ 49-a. Operation of a vessel while under the influence of alcohol or drugs 80

§ 49-b. Operating a vessel after having consumed alcohol; under the age of twenty-one; per se 95

§ 49-c. Termination of unsafe operation 105

§ 50. Owners to notify inspector and apply for inspection 106

§§ 51, 52. [Repealed] 106

§ 53. Rules and regulations 106

§ 54. Construction against fire 106

§ 55. Stairways and passageways 106

§ 56. Fire pump 107

§ 57. Identification number of vessel 108

§ 58. Number of passengers 108

§ 58-a. Unauthorized boarding of vessels 108

§ 59. Manning of public vessels 109

§ 60. Inability to provide licensed officer 109

§ 61. Repairs and modifications 109

§ 62. Loss of life by misconduct of officers 110

§ 63. Certificate of inspection 110

§ 64. Licenses 111

§ 64-a. Suspension and revocation of licenses 111

§ 65. Fees for vessel inspections and for the issuance of licenses 112

§ 66. Inflammable or explosive articles prohibited 112

§ 67. Public vessel equipment 113

§ 68. Investigations by inspector; penalties; reports 115

§ 69. Seizure of public vessels 115

§ 70. Minimum conditions for petroleum-bearing vessels in certain areas; tanker-avoidance zones ... 116

§ 70-a. Minimum conditions for petroleum-bearing vessels on the Hudson river; tanker-avoidance zones 117

§ 71. Petroleum-bearing vessel advisory commission 118

§§ 71, 71b. [Repealed] 119

§ 71-c. [Repealed] 119

§ 71-d. Liveries; safety regulations; penalty 119

§ 72. Operation of pleasure vessels on Round Island lake, Orange county 120

§ 72-a. Operation of vessels on the inland waters of Chautauqua county 120

§ 73. Towing of persons 120

§ 73-a. Regulations of personal watercraft and specialty prop-craft 121

§ 73-b. Misdemeanors 125

§ 73-c. Violations 125

§ 74. Service of summons and complaint on non-residents 126

§ 75. Educational program 128

§ 76. Information 129

§ 77. Rules and regulations 129

§ 78. Boating safety certificate 129

§ 78-a. Insurance rate reduction 129

§ 79. Courses of instruction 130

Article 4-A Enforcement by Counties *130*

§ 79-a. Definitions 130

§ 79-b. Vessel and equipment anti-theft program; eligibility for state aid 131

§ 79-c. Rules 133

Article 12 Oil Spill Prevention, Control, and Compensation *133*

§ 170. Legislative intent 133

§ 171. Purposes 134

§ 172. Definitions 134

§ 173. Discharge of petroleum; prohibition 137

§ 174. Licenses 138

§ 174-a. Use of containment booms 142

§ 174-b. Use of agents 143

§ 175. Notification by persons responsible for discharge 143

§ 176. Removal of prohibited discharges 143

§ 177. Emergency oil spill control network 147

§ 177-a. Emergency oil spill relocation network 148

§ 177-b. Habitat protection plan 149

§ 178. Right to enter and inspect 149

§ 178-a. Responder immunity 150

§ 179. New York environmental protection and spill compensation fund 152

§ 179-a. New York environmental protection and spill remediation account 153

§ 180. Administrator of the fund 153

§ 181. Liability 153

§ 181-a. Environmental lien 159

§ 181-b. Environmental lien notice; contents 160

§ 181-c. Filing of notice of environmental lien; filing of release 161

§ 181-d. Enforcement of environmental lien 161

§ 181-e. Amounts received to satisfy lien 161

§ 182. Claims against the fund 161

§ 183. Settlements 162

§ 184. Settlements when source of discharge is unknown 162

§ 185. Hearings for persons on claims filed with the administrator 162

§ 186. Disbursement of moneys from the fund 163

§ 187. Reimbursements of moneys to fund 165

§ 188. Subrogation of rights 165

§ 189. Awards exceeding current balance 166

§ 190. Claims against insurers 166

§ 190-a. Application of article 166

§ 191. Joint rules and regulations 166

§ 192. Enforcement of article; penalties 166

§ 193. Availability of additional remedies 167

§ 194. Severability 167

§ 195. Construction 167

§ 196. Reports 167

§ 197. Effect of federal legislation 167

Article 13 Miscellaneous Provisions; Saving Clause; Laws Repealed; When to Take Effect 168

§ 200. Collection of penalties 168

§ 201. Disposition of fees and penalties 169

§ 202. Application and saving clause...170

§ 203. Laws repealed..171

§ 204. When to take effect...171

Article 1 Short Title and Definitions

§ 1. Short title

This chapter shall be known as the navigation law, and shall apply to navigation and the use of navigable waters of the state and regulations hereby created.

§ 2. Definitions

The following terms when used in this chapter unless otherwise expressly stated, or unless the context of the language or subject matter indicates a different meaning or application was intended, shall be deemed to mean and include:

1. "Office" shall mean the state office of parks, recreation and historic preservation.

2. "Commissioner" shall mean the commissioner of parks, recreation and historic preservation, unless otherwise indicated, except that for purposes of the administration of articles three and eleven of this chapter within the sixth park region, the boundaries of which are described in subdivision six of section 7.01 of the parks, recreation and historic preservation law, "commissioner" shall mean the commissioner of environmental conservation.

3. [Repealed]

4. "Navigable waters of the state" shall mean all lakes, rivers, streams and waters within the boundaries of the state and not privately owned, which are navigable in fact or upon which vessels are operated, except all tidewaters bordering on and lying within the boundaries of Nassau and Suffolk counties.

5. "Navigable in fact" shall mean navigable in its natural or unimproved condition, affording a channel for useful commerce of a substantial and permanent character conducted in the customary mode of trade and travel on water. A theoretical or potential navigability, or one that is temporary, precarious and unprofitable is not sufficient, but to be navigable in fact a lake or stream must have practical usefulness to the public as a highway for transportation.

6. "Vessel" shall mean any floating craft and all vessels shall belong to one of the

following classes:

(a) "Public Vessel" shall mean and include every vessel which is propelled in whole or in part by mechanical power and is used or operated for commercial purposes on the navigable waters of the state; that is either carrying passengers, carrying freight, towing, or for any other use; for which a compensation is received, either directly or where provided as an accommodation, advantage, facility or privilege at any place of public accommodation, resort or amusement.

(b) "Residential vessel" shall mean and include every vessel which is used primarily as a residence.

(c) "Pleasure vessel" shall mean and include every vessel not within the classification of public vessel or residential vessel. However, the provisions of this chapter shall not apply to rowboats, canoes and kayaks except as otherwise expressly provided.

(d) The term "vessel" as used in this chapter shall not include a crew racing shell. "Crew racing shell" shall mean any shell, gig, barge or other boat designed primarily for practice or racing, propelled by oars or sweeps, in the sport of crew or scull racing conducted by a private or public educational institution, school, academy, college, university or association of any of the preceding, or by an amateur sports club or association or by the United States or International Olympics Committee and shall not include canoes, rowboats or lifeboats. The boat or launch accompanying a crew racing shell shall have sufficient safety devices to aid members of the crew should the need arise.

7. "Owner" shall mean the person actually holding title to a vessel, except a public vessel chartered unmanned for a period of more than thirty consecutive days, in which case "owner" shall include the person chartering the vessel.

8. "Person" shall mean an individual, partnership, corporation or association.

9. "Master" shall include every individual having for the time the charge, control or direction of a vessel.

10. "Pilot" shall mean an individual licensed to take charge of the course of a vessel through or upon specific waters.

11. "Engineer" shall mean an individual licensed to operate a vessel's main engines and auxiliaries.

12. "Joint pilot and engineer" shall mean an individual licensed to act as both pilot and engineer for a public vessel which in the judgment of the inspector can be safely navigated by one individual.

13. "Operator" shall mean an individual who operates or navigates a pleasure vessel.

14. "License" shall mean a certificate furnished by the inspector.

15. "Inspector" shall mean the individual, or individuals, provided for in article two, section twelve, of this chapter.

16. "Under way" shall mean that the vessel is not at anchor, or made fast to the shore, or aground.

17. "Visibility" as applied to lights shall mean discernibility on a dark night with a clear atmosphere.

18. "Starboard" shall mean the right hand side, facing the bow of the vessel.

19. "Port" shall mean the left hand side, facing the bow of the vessel.

20. "Wharf" shall mean and include any structure built or maintained for the purpose of providing a berthing place for vessels.

21. "Dock" shall mean a wharf, or portion of a wharf, extending along the shore line and generally connected with the uplands throughout its length.

22. "Pier" shall mean a wharf or portion of a wharf extending from the shore line with water on both sides.

23. "Jetty" shall mean a structure located within the shore lines of a body of water for the purpose of controlling currents usually to prevent filling in a channel.

24. "Breakwater" shall mean a structure located within the shore line of a body of water for the purpose of providing protection from wind and wave action.

25. "Undocumented vessel" shall mean any vessel which is not required to have, and does not have, a valid marine document issued by the federal bureau of customs.

26. "Open construction" shall mean that a vessel is so constructed as to be void of any decking or enclosure which inhibits the continuous and free circulation of air within the vessel when under way.

27. "Aids to navigation" shall mean buoys, beacons or other fixed objects in the water which are used to mark obstructions to navigation or to direct navigation through safe

channels.

28. "Floating objects" shall mean any anchored marker or platform floating on the surface of the water other than aids to navigation and shall include but not be limited to, bathing beach markers, speed zone markers, information markers, swimming or diving floats, mooring buoys, fishing buoys, and ski jumps.

29. "Gray water" shall mean waste water generated by water using fixtures other than toilets; including but not limited to baths, sinks and laundry facilities used on residential vessels.

30. "Personal watercraft" shall mean a vessel which uses an inboard motor powering a water jet pump as its primary source of motive power and which is designed to be operated by a person sitting, standing, or kneeling on, or being towed behind the vessel rather than in the conventional manner of sitting or standing inside the vessel.

30-a. "Personal flotation device" shall mean a wearable flotation device, classified and approved by the United States Coast Guard which is in such a condition that it is fit for its intended purpose, bears a legibly marked United States Coast Guard approval number and is of an appropriate size for the person who intends to use it.

31. "Specialty prop-craft" shall mean a vessel which is powered by an outboard motor or a propeller driven motor and which is designed to be operated by a person sitting, standing or kneeling on or being towed behind the vessel rather than in the conventional manner of sitting or standing inside the vessel.

32. "Effective muffler" or "underwater exhaust system" shall mean a sound suppression device or system designed and installed to abate the sound of exhaust gases emitted from an internal combustion engine and which prevents excessive or unusual noise, as set forth in section forty-four of this chapter.

33. "Abandoned historic shipwreck" shall mean wrecks situated on or under lands owned by the state, in which the state holds title pursuant to the Abandoned Shipwrecks Act of 1987 (43 U.S.C. 2101) or which, by reason of their antiquity, history, architecture, archaeology or cultural value, have state or national importance and are eligible for inclusion on the state register of historic places, and which have been abandoned by the owner of record. The term shall include the wreck, its cargo and contents and the situs.

34. "Wreck" shall mean any wrecked property, other than an abandoned historic shipwreck.

Article 2 Administration

§ 10. Duties of the commissioner of parks, recreation and historic preservation and the commissioner of environmental conservation

The commissioner of parks, recreation and historic preservation shall administer the provisions of this chapter, except as such administration may be otherwise provided. He or she may delegate such administration to another officer or employee of the office of parks, recreation and historic preservation. Within the sixth park region, the boundaries of which are described in subdivision six of section 7.01 of the parks, recreation and historic preservation law, the commissioner of environmental conservation shall administer the provisions of articles three and eleven of this chapter. He or she may delegate such administration to another officer or employee of the department of environmental conservation.

§ 11. [Repealed]

§ 12. Inspector; qualifications

The commissioner may appoint an inspector or inspectors, who shall have a practical knowledge of the construction, equipment and management of vessels and who shall possess such experience and qualifications as required to carry out and fulfill the duties of inspector indicated in this chapter and specifically defined in section thirteen hereof and as may be determined by the New York state civil service department.

§ 13. Inspector; duties

The inspector shall annually, and at such other times as he shall deem it expedient, or as the commissioner may direct, inspect every public vessel, except vessels which navigate on waters over which the United States exercises active control. The inspector shall carefully examine the hull, the propelling and auxiliary machinery, the electrical apparatus and the vessel's equipment. He shall require such changes, repairs and improvements to be made as he may deem expedient for the contemplated route. No vessel, or propelling machinery thereof shall be allowed to be used if constructed in whole, or in part, of defective material, or which because of its form, design, workmanship, age, use or for any other reason is unsafe. He shall also fix the number of passengers that may be transported. The inspector shall require that the boilers, on all public vessels which are propelled by steam engines, be inspected and approved for safety of operations by inspectors of the New York State Department of Labor, Bureau of Boilers. Every boiler and appurtenances thereof shall be constructed, maintained and operated in accordance with the Department of Labor rules and regulations pertaining to boilers. The inspector shall also, whenever he deems it expedient, visit any vessel licensed under this chapter and examine into her condition for the purpose of ascertaining whether or not any party thereon, having a certificate, or license, from the inspector, has conformed to and obeyed the conditions of such certificate, and the provisions of this chapter. The owner, master, pilot, engineer or joint pilot and engineer of such vessel, shall answer all reasonable questions and give all the information in his or their power in regard to said vessel, or its machinery or equipment and the manner of managing the same. The inspector provided for in this chapter is authorized to make further rules and regulations applying generally to all vessels, or especially to one or more of them. In framing rules for the government of managers and employees on vessels, the inspector shall, as far as practicable, be governed by the general rules and regulations prescribed by the United States coast guard. The inspector shall have the power to issue a uniform navigation summons and/or complaint for violations of the provisions of article four of this chapter which are applicable to vessels.

§ 14. Inspector; licenses

The inspector is authorized and empowered to grant licenses as provided in article four of this chapter.

§ 15. Inspector; fees

The inspector is authorized to collect fees as provided in article four of this chapter.

§ 16. Inspector; reports

The inspector shall on or about the first day of January in each year, make a verified report to the commissioner containing a detailed statement of the name and registry number of each vessel examined and licensed, the name and registry number of each vessel to which license was refused and stating the reasons for refusal, the name of each person examined and licensed, the name of each person to whom license was refused and stating the reason therefor, and may include in such report any other information the inspector deems desirable.

§ 17. Traveling navigation inspectors

The commissioner may appoint not to exceed three traveling navigation inspectors whose qualifications shall include a full knowledge of the navigation law and regulations established thereunder and a practical experience in the navigation of vessels. Such inspectors shall be employed for such periods of the year and at such rates of pay as the commissioner may deem necessary, and shall have the power to issue a uniform navigation summons and/or complaint for violations of the provisions of article four of this chapter which are applicable to vessels.

§ 18. Special navigation inspectors

The commissioner may, if in his judgment conditions so require, appoint members of local boat clubs, or other persons found competent, to act as special navigation inspectors during regattas authorized by him. The power and authority in such special navigation inspectors shall be limited to the period during which the regatta is authorized and to the enforcement of the navigation law and special regulations. Upon the completion of the regatta, he shall file with the commissioner a report covering the conduct of the regatta and his activities. Such special navigation inspector shall receive no compensation from the state. Any expense in connection with his duties shall be borne by the person conducting the regatta.

§ 19. Uniform navigation summons and complaint

1. The commissioner shall be authorized to prescribe the form of summons and/or complaint in all cases involving a violation of any provision of this chapter or of any ordinance, rule or regulation relating to navigation, or of any class or category of such cases, and to establish procedures for proper administrative controls over the disposition thereof. The provisions of this subdivision shall not apply to offenses specified in paragraph b of subdivision four of section forty-nine of this chapter.

2. The chief executive officer of each local police force including county, town, city and village police departments, sheriffs, and the superintendent of state police shall prepare or

cause to be prepared such records and reports as may be prescribed hereunder.

3. The commissioner shall have the power from time to time to adopt such rules and regulations as may be necessary to accomplish the purposes and enforce the provisions of this section including requirements for reporting by trial courts having jurisdiction over navigation violations.

4. The provisions of this section shall not apply to or supersede any ordinance, rule or regulation heretofore or hereafter made, adopted or prescribed pursuant to law in Nassau or Suffolk counties or in any city having a population of one million or over.

5. Any person who disposes of any uniform navigation summons and/or complaint in any manner other than that prescribed by law, rule or regulation shall be guilty of a misdemeanor.

6. If a person charged with a violation desires to plead guilty to the violation as charged in the summons, he shall submit to the magistrate having jurisdiction, in person, by duly authorized agent or by registered mail, a verified application or in lieu thereof, an application affirmed under penalty of perjury setting forth (a) the nature of the charge, (b) the violations, if any, of the navigation law or of any local law or ordinance governing or regulating navigation, of which the defendant has been convicted within a period of two years immediately preceding the date of the impending charge, together with the date, the name and place of the court and the disposition, with respect to each violation, (c) the information or instructions required by section one thousand eight hundred seven of the vehicle and traffic law to be given defendant upon arraignment, (d) that defendant waives arraignment in open court and the aid of counsel, (e) that he pleads guilty to the offense as charged, (f) that defendant elects and requests that the charge be disposed of and the fine or penalty fixed by the court, pursuant to this subdivision, and (g) any statement or explanation that the defendant may desire to make concerning the offense charged. The application shall be in such form as the commissioner shall prescribe and a copy thereof shall be handed to the defendant by the person charging him with such violation. Thereupon the magistrate may proceed as though the defendant had been convicted upon a plea of guilty in open court, provided, however, that any imposition of fine or penalty hereunder, without suspension of execution of sentence, shall be deemed tentative until such fine or penalty shall have been paid and discharged in full, prior to which time the magistrate, in his discretion, may annul

any proceedings hereunder, including such tentative imposition of fine or penalty, and deny the application, in which event the charge shall be disposed of pursuant to the applicable provisions of law, as though no proceedings had been had under this subdivision. If upon receipt of the aforesaid application the magistrate shall deny the same, he shall thereupon inform the defendant of this fact, and that he is required to appear before the said magistrate at a stated time and place to answer the charge which shall thereafter be disposed of pursuant to the applicable provisions of law.

§ 20. Verification of complaints

Where a navigation summons has been served by a peace officer, acting pursuant to his special duties, police officer, or traveling navigation inspector, in cases of violations of any provision of this chapter or of any ordinance, rule or regulation enacted pursuant thereto or pursuant to any other law relating to navigation, any chief, deputy-chief, captain, lieutenant or acting lieutenant, sergeant or acting sergeant of a police department, or any sheriff, undersheriff, chief deputy, deputy sergeant or deputy in charge of navigation maintained by any sheriff in any county to whom the service of the navigation summons is reported, is hereby authorized to administer to such officer or traveling navigation inspector, all necessary oaths in connection with the execution of the complaint to be presented in court by such officer or traveling navigation inspector, in the prosecution of such offense but a complaint need not be verified provided it shall be affirmed under penalty of perjury.

Article 3 Navigable Waters of the State

§ 30. Navigation, jurisdiction over

The commissioner shall have jurisdiction over navigation on the navigable waters of the state and, except as otherwise provided, shall enforce the provisions of this chapter and the regulations established thereunder. As a guide to the interpretation and application of this article, nothing authorized hereunder shall be construed to convey any property rights, either in real estate or material, or any exclusive privilege; nor authorize any injury to private property or invasion of private rights or any infringement of federal, state or local laws or regulations, but shall express the assent of the state so far as it concerns the public rights of navigation. Nothing contained in this section shall be construed to limit, impair or affect the general powers and duties of the canal corporation relating to canals as set forth in section ten of the canal law.

§ 31. Excavation, fill or other modification of water course

No person or local public corporation shall excavate or place fill in the navigable waters of the state without first obtaining a permit therefor in conformity with the provisions of section 15-0505 of the environmental conservation law.

§ 32. Location of structures in or on navigable waters

1. Notwithstanding the provisions of subdivision two of section forty-six-a of this chapter, no wharf, dock, pier, jetty, platform or other structure built on floats, columns, open timber, piles or similar open-work supports, temporary or permanent, shall be constructed, installed, repaired, modified, expanded or otherwise placed by any person in the navigable waters of the state or in a navigable channel or replaced by any person in such waters or channel on or after the effective date of this section after having been removed from such waters or channel for a period in excess of thirty days so as to interfere with the free and direct access to such waters from the property, wharf, dock or similar structure of any other person unless written permission is obtained therefor from such other person.

2. In case any written complaint shall be filed with the commissioner of general services and he shall have cause to believe, or in case the commissioner himself shall have cause to believe, that any person is violating the provisions of this section or any rule or regulation promulgated pursuant to this section, the commissioner shall cause a prompt investigation to be made.

3. The commissioner shall have the power, after hearing on due notice, to make and serve an order, setting forth the findings of fact and conclusions therefrom, directing any person constructing, installing, repairing, modifying, expanding or otherwise placing or using any such structure to either move or remove the said structure or to reconstruct, repair or modify the same within such reasonable time and in such manner as shall be specified in said order, and it shall be the duty of every such person to obey, observe and comply with such order and the conditions therein prescribed. The commissioner is authorized to adopt, amend, repeal and enforce such rules and regulations as he may deem necessary to govern

administrative procedures applicable to hearings under this section.

4. It shall be unlawful for any person to fail, omit or neglect to comply with such order or to fail to move, remove, reconstruct, repair or modify said structure as provided in the order within a reasonable time as designated by the commissioner.

5. Any person who fails, omits or neglects to comply with or otherwise violates any such order shall be liable for a civil penalty of not more than one hundred dollars for such violation and an additional civil penalty of not more than one hundred dollars for each day during which such violation continues, to be assessed by the commissioner.

6. The commissioner is hereby authorized to commence an action or proceeding in a court of competent jurisdiction to compel compliance with any order made and to recover any penalty assessed pursuant to the provisions of this section.

7. Any civil penalty or order issued by the commissioner under this section shall be reviewable in a proceeding under article seventy-eight of the civil practice law and rules.

8. The provisions of this section shall not apply to marine terminals including piers, wharves, docks, bulkheads, slips, basins and other structures or facilities used in the transportation of waterborne cargo or passengers in interstate or foreign commerce.

§ 32-a. Using net or weir unlawfully in Hudson river

A person, who uses any net or weir for setting or attaching nets, or a pole or other fixture in any part of the Hudson river, except as permitted by statute, is guilty of a misdemeanor.

§ 32-b. Lights upon swing bridges

A corporation, company, or individual, owning, maintaining or operating a swing bridge across the Hudson river, who during the navigation season between sundown and sunrise, neglects to keep and maintain upon every such bridge the lights required by law, is guilty of a misdemeanor.

§ 32-c. Interfering with navigation

A person who throws, or causes, or permits to be thrown, from any boat, scow, or other vessel, or in any other manner, into the tidewaters bordering on or lying within the boundaries of Nassau and Suffolk counties or any of the navigable waters of this state, including bays, sounds and harbors, any earth, ashes, cinders, stone, or other material, or who builds any structure therein, which will in any manner lessen the depth of such waters, or interfere with the free and safe navigation thereof, is guilty of a misdemeanor.

§ 32-d. Dumping or depositing of certain materials in the Genesee river

Except as specifically authority [authorized]* by law, no person shall dump or deposit, or allow to be dumped or deposited, logs, lumber, timber, fabricated wood products or wood debris in the Genesee river which may interfere with the free and safe navigation thereof. A violation of the provisions hereof shall be a misdemeanor punishable by a fine of not to exceed one hundred dollars, or by imprisonment of not more than thirty days, or by both such fine and imprisonment.

§ 32-e. Restriction and regulation of structures in certain towns and villages in the county of Niagara

The local legislative body of the towns of Lewiston and Porter and the villages of Youngstown and Lewiston for the purpose of responsible shoreline management, may adopt, amend and enforce local laws, rules and regulations not inconsistent with the laws of this state or of the United States, with respect to the restriction and regulation of the manner of construction and location of structures in the Niagara River within or bounding the towns of Lewiston and Porter and the villages of Youngstown and Lewiston to a distance of one-half the width of the river or up to the United States-Canadian border. Structures may include boathouses, wharfs, piers, docks, jetties or other types of structures which are non-permanent in nature or which are otherwise not subject to permit requirements.

§ 33. Deposit of refuse in navigable waters of the state

No person shall drain, deposit or cast any dead animal, carrion, offal, excrement, garbage or other putrid or offensive matter into the navigable waters of the state or any tidewaters bordering on or lying within the boundaries of Nassau and Suffolk counties, except as the same may be authorized by the state department of health. Every person violating the provisions of this section shall upon conviction by any court of competent jurisdiction be guilty of a misdemeanor punishable by a fine of not to exceed one hundred dollars, or by imprisonment of not more than one year, or by both such fine and imprisonment for each offense. The district attorney of the county, in which the offense is committed or exists, is authorized and directed to prosecute such offender or offenders.

§ 33-a. Sanitary facilities aboard craft on Lake George, Canandaigua Lake, Keuka Lake, Skaneateles Lake and on Greenwood Lake, Orange county

It shall be unlawful for any owner or operator or for a marina or other business to launch, moor, dock or operate any craft, or permit such launching, mooring or operating of any craft upon Lake George, upon Canandaigua Lake, upon Keuka Lake, upon Skaneateles Lake, and upon Greenwood Lake, Orange county, their tributaries or outlets, equipped with toilets, sinks, tubs, showers, or other equipment resulting in the drainage of waste water or other sanitary facilities which in any manner discharge into the waters of the lake, its tributaries or outlet. All such toilets, sinks, tubs, showers, or other equipment resulting in the drainage of waste water, or other sanitary facilities, shall be removed or sealed or made to drain into a tank or reservoir which can be carried or pumped ashore for disposal according to the regulations of local boards of health or county and state health agencies. Failure to comply with the provisions of this section aboard craft on Lake George, Canandaigua Lake, Keuka Lake, and on Greenwood Lake, Orange county shall be a misdemeanor punishable by a fine of not to exceed one hundred dollars, or by imprisonment of not more than one year, or by both such fine and imprisonment. Failure to comply with the provisions of this section aboard craft on Skaneateles Lake shall be a misdemeanor punishable by a fine not to exceed five hundred dollars, or by imprisonment of not more than one year, or by both such fine and imprisonment.

§ 33-b. Dumping or depositing trash and other debris in Chautauqua lake and its tributaries; ice fishing shanties on lakes within the state of New York; identification of duck blinds

Any person who dumps, deposits or allows or causes to be dumped or deposited in any manner any trash, glass, bottles, garbage or any other debris in the waters of Chautauqua lake or its tributaries, or upon the shore line adjacent thereto, or upon the ice covering the waters of Chautauqua lake, or any person who constructs, moves, places or causes or allows to be constructed, moved or placed any structure upon the ice covering the waters of lakes within the state of New York, shall be guilty of, a violation punishable by a fine of not to exceed one hundred dollars, unless the person who constructs, moves, places or causes or allows to be constructed, moved or placed any structure upon the ice covering the waters of lakes within the state of New York shall have placed thereon with paint or in some other permanent manner the owner's full name in characters at least three inches high and his address in a contrasting color to the surrounding structure, and provided further the said structure is removed not later than the fifteenth day of March in each year or such other date as may be set by the department of environmental conservation. Every duck blind, placed in the waters of lakes within the state of New York, shall have prominently placed thereon, in some permanent manner, the owner's full name and address, and further each duck blind so placed shall be removed from the water no later than the fifteenth day of March following its placement. The wilful failure of an owner of a duck blind to affix such identification or remove it from the water by the prescribed date shall subject said owner to a fine of one hundred dollars.

§ 33-c. Regulating disposal of sewage; littering of waterways

1. As used in this section, unless the context clearly indicates otherwise:

(a) The term "watercraft" means any contrivance used or capable of being used for navigation upon water whether or not capable of self-propulsion, except passenger or cargo-carrying vessels subject to the Quarantine Regulations of the United States Public Health Service adopted pursuant to Title forty-two of the United States Code.

(b) The term "marina" means any installation which provides any accommodations or facilities for watercraft, including mooring, docking, storing, leasing, sale, or servicing of watercraft, located adjacent to waters of the state.

(c) The term "sewage" means all human body wastes.

(d) The term "litter" means any bottles, glass, crockery, cans, scrap metal, junk, paper, garbage, rubbish, trash, or similar refuse.

(e) The term "marine toilet" means any toilet on or within any watercraft, except those that have been permanently sealed and made inoperative.

(f) The term "waters of this state" means all of the waterways, or bodies of water located within New York state or that part of any body of water which is adjacent to New York state over which the state has territorial jurisdictions on which watercraft may be used or operated.

(g) The term "person" means an individual, partnership, firm, corporation, association, or other entity.

(h) The term "department" means the state department of environmental conservation, except as otherwise provided in this section.

(i) The term "marine holding tank" means any container aboard any vessel that is designed and used for the purpose of collecting and storing treated or untreated sewage from marine toilets.

(j) The term "pumpout facility" means any device, portable or permanent, capable of removing sewage from a marine holding tank.

2.

(a) No person, whether engaged in commerce or otherwise, shall place, throw, deposit, or discharge, or cause to be placed, thrown, deposited, or discharged into the waters of this state, from any watercraft, marina or mooring, any sewage, or other liquid or solid materials which render the water unsightly, noxious or otherwise unwholesome so as to be detrimental to the public health or welfare or to the enjoyment of the water for recreational purposes.

(b) No person, whether engaged in commerce or otherwise, shall place, throw, deposit or discharge, or cause to be placed, thrown, deposited, or discharged, any litter into the waters of this state or upon any public lands contiguous to and within one hundred feet of such waters or upon any private lands contiguous to and within one hundred feet of such waters unless such lands are owned by such person or unless such person enters or remains with the permission of the owner of record or his representative or agent.

3.

(a) No marine toilet on any watercraft used or operated upon waters of this state shall be operated so as to discharge any untreated sewage into said waters directly or indirectly.

(b) No person owning or operating a watercraft with a marine toilet shall use, or permit the use of, such toilet on the waters of this state unless the toilet is equipped with facilities that will adequately treat, hold, incinerate or otherwise handle sewage in a manner that is capable of preventing water pollution, as required by this section.

(c) Except as provided in subdivisions four and seven of this section, no container of sewage shall be placed, left, discharged or caused to be placed, left or discharged in or bordering any waters of this state by any person at any time.

4.

(a) Every marine toilet on watercraft used or operated upon the waters of this state shall be equipped with a pollution control device, either for the treatment or holding of sewage, in operating condition, of a type approved by the state health department, in conformance with applicable public health standards and rules and regulations; and approved by the department in conformance with the boating safety standards and rules and regulations adopted by the department. Pollution control devices shall be securely affixed to the interior discharge opening of marine toilets and all sewage passing into or through such toilets shall pass solely through such treatment facilities.

(b) Sewage passing through a marine toilet equipped with a chlorinator or chemical treatment facility shall be deemed untreated unless the effluent meets standards established by the state commissioner of health.

(c) The disinfecting agent used in the facility shall be of a kind which when discharged as a part of the effluent is not toxic to humans, fish or wildlife.

(d) The active ingredient in deodorizers used in marine toilets may only consist of formaldehyde, enzymes, bacterial cultures or any other ingredient which would not interfere with the operation of sewage treatment plants. No zinc or other heavy metal or phenol may be used in any marine toilet.

5. No marine toilet pollution control device shall be used, sold or physically offered for sale in this state unless it is of a type which has officially been approved by the department. The department approval shall be issued only after approval of such devices by the state department of health, as required by subdivision four of this section. Notice of such approval may be required by the department to be displayed on the pollution control device.

6. The department shall require persons making application for a boat registration certificate for a watercraft pursuant to section seventy-one of the navigation law to disclose whether such watercraft has within or on it a marine toilet, and if so, to certify that such toilet is equipped with a pollution control device as required by this section. The department is further empowered to direct that the issuance of a boat registration certificate or a renewal thereof be withheld if such device had not been installed as provided in this section.

7. The owner or whoever is lawfully vested with the possession, management or control of a marina shall be required to provide suitable trash receptacles or similar devices designed for the depositing of litter at locations where they can be conveniently utilized by watercraft

users.

8. All marinas that provide pumpout facilities and dump stations for the handling and disposal of sewage from marine holding tanks and portable toilets shall do so in a manner that will prevent the pollution of the surface waters of the state. The facilities for unloading and disposal of such sewage shall be approved by either the local or the state health department in accordance with guidelines set forth by the department in consultation with the department of health. The department of environmental conservation shall require that municipal sewage treatment facilities accept such waste originating from marine holding tanks and portable toilets unless the commissioner determines that such action would cause an unacceptable threat to human health or the environment or the operation of a sewage treatment plant.

9. All watercraft located upon waters of this state shall be subject to boarding and inspection by the department or health department or any lawfully designated agents or inspectors thereof, for the purpose of determining whether such watercraft is equipped with approved marina toilet pollution control facilities operated in compliance herewith.

10. Any municipality within which a vessel waste no-discharge zone has been designated pursuant to subdivision one of section thirty-three-e of this article or any municipality adjacent to which a vessel waste no-discharge zone has been designated pursuant to subdivision one of section thirty-three-e of this article, may adopt and enforce local laws, not inconsistent with section thirty-three-e of this article, prohibiting the discharge of vessel wastes in waters within such municipality, or in waters adjacent to such municipality to a distance of one thousand five hundred feet from shore. Nothing in this section shall preclude the political subdivisions of Nassau and Suffolk counties from regulating gray water discharge from residential vessels moored on tidewaters bordering on and lying within the boundaries of Nassau or Suffolk county.

11. The department is hereby authorized and empowered to make, adopt, promulgate, amend and repeal such standards and rules and regulations as are necessary, or convenient for the carrying out of duties and obligations and powers conferred on the department by this section.

12. A copy of the regulations adopted pursuant to this section and any of the amendments

thereto, shall be filed in the office of the department, the health department, the water resources commission, and in the office of the secretary of state. Rules and regulations and standards shall be published by the department in convenient form.

13.

(a) Any person who violates paragraph (b) of subdivision two of this section, shall be guilty of an offense and upon conviction shall be punished with a fine of not more than two hundred fifty dollars, or by imprisonment of not more than sixty days, or by both such fine and imprisonment; provided, however, that in the event any person violates this section more than twice during the same calendar year and is convicted of more than two such violations, the third and each subsequent violation shall be deemed a misdemeanor.

(b) Any person who violates any other provision of this section or regulations of the department adopted pursuant hereto shall be deemed guilty of a misdemeanor and upon conviction shall be punished with a fine of not more than one hundred dollars, or by imprisonment of not more than sixty days, or by both such fine and imprisonment.

14. Any action taken by the department or the state department of health pursuant to subdivisions five or six of this section shall be subject to review by the supreme court in the manner provided by article seventy-eight of the civil practice law and rules provided that no stay shall be granted pending the determination of the matter except on notice to the department and the state department of health and for a period not exceeding thirty days. Proceedings to review any action enumerated herein shall be entitled to a preference.

15. If any court shall find any subdivision or subdivisions of this section to be unconstitutional or otherwise invalid, such findings shall not affect the validity of any sections of this act which can be given effect.

16. Nothing in this section, shall be deemed to repeal, amend, modify or alter the provisions of article twelve of the public health law or the provisions of sections thirty-three-a and thirty-three-b of the navigation law.

§ 33-d. Sanitary facilities aboard crafts on Lake Champlain

It shall be unlawful for any owner or operator of any craft upon Lake Champlain, its tributaries or outlets, to operate any craft equipped with a marine toilet which in any manner discharges sewage into the waters of said lake, its tributaries or outlets. All marine toilets on any such craft shall also incorporate or be equipped with a holding tank which can be carried or pumped ashore for disposal according to the regulations of local boards of health or county or state health agencies. Any holding tank designed so as to provide for an optional means of discharge to the waters on which the craft is operating shall have the discharge openings sealed shut and any discharge lines, pipes or hoses shall be removed or disconnected and stored while operating on the waters of said lake, its tributaries or outlets. Failure to comply with the provisions of this section shall be a violation punishable by a fine not to exceed two hundred fifty dollars or by imprisonment of not more than fifteen days or by both such fine and imprisonment.

§ 33-e. Marine sanitation devices aboard vessels in vessel waste no-discharge zones

1. Any waters of the state of which the commissioner has received an affirmative determination regarding the adequate availability of marine sanitation device pump-out or dump station facilities pursuant to the Federal Clean Water Act, are hereby designated as vessel waste no-discharge zones.

2. It shall be unlawful for any operator or person in control of a vessel being operated upon any waters of the state designated as vessel waste no-discharge zones to discharge sewage from marine toilets into such waters. Any marine sanitation device on board any vessel being operated in such waters must be secured to prevent any marine sanitation device discharges to such waters. In accordance with federal requirements, any marine sanitation device aboard any vessel being operated upon any waters within such vessel waste no-discharge zone shall be secured by closing the seacock and padlocking, using a non-releasable wire-tie, removing the seacock handle or locking the door to the "head" while such vessel is being operated upon waters within vessel waste no-discharge zones. If a marine sanitation device on any such vessel provides a means of discharging sewage directly to such waters, the discharge valve must be secured in a readily visible manner and closed position while the vessel is being operated upon such waters.

Use of a padlock, heavy non-resealable tape, wire-tie, or the removal of the valve handle are adequate methods of securing the device. The method chosen shall be one that presents a physical barrier to the use of the valve. It is unlawful for any person operating or in control of a vessel with a marine sanitation device on board to operate or control such vessel in a vessel waste no-discharge zone when the marine sanitation device is not secured in the manner described herein.

3. The provisions of subdivision two of this section, requiring that marine sanitation devices be rendered inoperable, shall not apply while the wastes from the marine sanitation device are being lawfully disposed of in an approved marine sanitation device pump-out or dump station located within a vessel waste no-discharge zone.

4. Any vessel being operated upon waters of the state that have been designated as vessel waste no-discharge zones may be boarded and inspected by the department or health department or any lawfully designated agents or inspectors thereof, acting pursuant to their special duties in accordance with subdivision nine of section thirty-three-c of this article for the purpose of determining whether such vessel is being operated in compliance with this section.

5. Failure to comply with the provisions of this section shall be a violation punishable by a fine not to exceed five hundred dollars. Any subsequent failure by the same operator or person in control of a vessel to comply with the provisions of this section shall be a violation punishable by a fine not to exceed one thousand dollars.

§ 34. Regattas

The commissioner may authorize the holding of regattas or boat races on any navigable waters of the state within his jurisdiction. He shall adopt and may, from time to time, amend regulations concerning the safety of vessels and the passengers and other persons thereon, either observers or participants. Whenever a regatta or boat race is proposed to be held on such waters, the person in charge thereof, shall, at least fifteen days prior thereto, file an application with the commissioner in his office at Albany for permission to hold such regatta or boat race. The application shall set forth the date and location where it is proposed to hold such regatta or boat races and it shall not be conducted without authorization of the commissioner in writing. A copy of the regulations adopted pursuant to this section, and of any amendments thereto, shall be filed in the office of the commissioner and in the office of the department of state. A copy of such regulations shall be furnished by the commissioner to any person making due application therefor. Any person who shall violate any regulation adopted pursuant to this section shall for every such violation forfeit to the people of the state the sum of not to exceed two hundred and fifty dollars to be recovered in a civil action.

§ 34-a. Permits for racing shell regattas not required

Nothing contained in section thirty-four of this chapter or in any other general or special law shall be deemed or construed as requiring any permit or permission to hold a regatta or race of rowing shells by any educational institution or amateur rowing organization in navigable waters of the state. For the purpose of this section, a "racing shell" is defined to mean any boat, specially designed for racing and propelled solely by means of oars, not including lifeboats or standard type rowboats, not specifically designed for rowing races. Any educational institution or amateur rowing organization, however, shall file with the commissioner a notification of all races to be held, setting forth the dates, places, a description of the course and the number of entrants in each race. No fee shall be charged for such filing.

§ 35. Aids to navigation

The commissioner may authorize, through the issuance of a revocable permit, the placing of aids to navigation in the navigable waters of the state, and any tidewaters bordering on or lying within the boundaries of Nassau and Suffolk counties, to mark obstructions to navigation, or for any other purpose, if, in his judgment, it will promote safety of navigation. Any person interested in the navigation of the navigable waters of the state, and any tidewaters bordering on or lying within the boundaries of Nassau and Suffolk counties, who may desire to place such aids to navigation therein, without expense to the state, may make application to the commissioner and submit a map suitable for blue print reproduction showing the proposed location of such aids to navigation and their color and meaning. The commissioner shall make rules and regulations establishing the size, shape, color and significance of such aids to navigation. When authorization has been granted the said aids to navigation shall be deemed lawfully placed. If, in the judgment of the commissioner, aids to navigation authorized by him are found to be improperly placed or that the reason for their placement no longer exists, he may revoke the permit authorizing their placement by written notice mailed to the person to whom the permit was issued directing their removal within a specified time. The person to whom such notice is directed shall thereupon remove the aids to navigation in accordance with such instructions. In case of failure by the person so directed to remove the aids to navigation within the specified time, the commissioner may cause their removal. The cost and expense of such removal shall be a charge against the person authorized to place the aids to navigation and it shall be recoverable through action in any court of competent jurisdiction. Each aid to navigation lawfully placed shall bear in a conspicuous place and in legible condition the letters "NYS". Any person placing such designating letters on an aid to navigation not lawfully placed, in accordance with this section, shall be guilty of a misdemeanor and upon conviction by a court of competent jurisdiction shall be subject to a fine of not more than twenty-five dollars for each and every offense. Any person who shall moor or fasten a vessel to a lawfully placed aid to navigation or shall wilfully damage, alter the location of, or otherwise render ineffective a lawfully placed aid to navigation shall be guilty of a misdemeanor and upon conviction before a court of competent jurisdiction shall be subject to a fine of not more than fifty dollars for each and every offense.

§ 35-a. Floating objects other than aids to navigation

1. The commissioner may authorize, through the issuance of a revocable permit, the placing in the navigable waters of the state, of mooring buoys, bathing beach markers, swimming floats, speed zone markers, or any other floating object having no navigational significance, if in his opinion the placing of such floating object will not be a hazard to navigation.

2. The commissioner is hereby authorized to make rules and regulations for the issuance of such permits and he shall establish a uniform system of marking all floating objects that he authorizes to be placed.

3. Adjacent upland owners may place one mooring buoy and one swimming float of not more than one hundred square feet of surface area, in the waters adjacent to and within the boundaries of their shoreline, provided however, that no floating object and no vessel or part thereof which is secured to a mooring buoy shall at any time extend more than one hundred feet from shore and further provided that no floating object may be placed in a navigable channel or in any location in which it will interfere with free and safe navigation or free access to another person's property. The commissioner shall have the right to remove or alter the location of any such buoy or float in the interest of navigation.

4. The commissioner may, by rule, regulation, or order, designate lakes, or areas within lakes, in which fishing buoys may be placed. The commissioner shall specify the size, shape, color and material of construction for such buoys, the manner of placing same and the type of ground tackle to be used. No fishing buoys may be placed in the navigable waters of the state except as specified by the commissioner in rules and regulations authorized herein.

5. The commissioner may prescribe a reasonable service charge to cover the cost of issuance of permits authorized by this section. Revenues from such service charges shall be deposited into the "I love NY waterways" boating safety fund established pursuant to section ninety-seven-nn of the state finance law.

6. The provisions of this section which pertain to the mooring of vessels shall not apply to areas in which local ordinances so pertaining have been duly approved by the commissioner or in which areas federal laws or rules and regulations regulate the anchoring or mooring of vessels.

7. A violation of this section or the rules and regulations authorized herein shall constitute an offense punishable by a fine of not to exceed fifty dollars.

§ 35-b. Markers for skin or scuba divers

1. The commissioner is hereby authorized to make rules and regulations requiring the use of a red flag with a diagonal white bar to be displayed on the water or from a boat by skin divers or scuba divers which would indicate underwater diving and significantly mark their position in such waters. The commissioner shall specify the size, shape, material of construction and manner of placing such markers.

2. A violation of such rules and regulations so established pursuant to subdivision one herein, shall constitute an offense punishable by a fine not to exceed fifty dollars.

§ 35-c. Real time and wind water level telemetry system

1. Establishment of system. The secage retary of state shall arrange for the establishment of a real time and wind water level telemetry system to inform and assist users of the harbors and waterways of the state.

2. General functions and powers. To provide for such a real time and wind water level telemetry system, the department of state shall have the power, duty and authority:

a. To arrange for the construction, installation, operation and maintenance of a computerized information system based on water level gauges and other remote sensing devices, starting from lower New York harbor and the lower Hudson river to Haverstraw bay and the Albany area and including the entrance to Long Island sound extending, as user demand may warrant, to other ports and waterways of the state;

b. To arrange for the establishment of a schedule of fees to be charged to actual users for the information provided from such a system, adequate to amortize the cost of installation and construction, to recover the annual costs of operation and maintenance and to collect such fees; and

c. To report annually to the governor and the legislature on the operation of the program for the year preceding and plans and recommendations for the future.

3. Specific functions. To carry out this program the department of state may:

a. Develop and promulgate orders, rules and regulations to effectuate the purposes of this section;

b. Contract with public or private organizations to perform the various activities required by this section, including construction, operation, maintenance, collection of fees and monitoring of the program;

c. Designate employees of the department of state who shall be empowered to examine the records of such contractors as to the collection and expenditure of funds;

d. Apply for, accept and expend any federal or other monies made available for the purposes of this section;

e. Require and receive assistance from any agency of the state or any political subdivision thereof in the furtherance of this program;

f. Act as the agent of the state, when required by this program, in arrranging cooperative agreements with other states and Canada; and

g. Set up an advisory committee of experts and representatives of other public and private agencies to facilitate the program's execution.

§ 35-d. Aquatic invasive species signs at public boat launches

1. The department of environmental conservation shall design and establish universal signage which may be posted at any access point to the navigable waters of the state relating to the threat and mitigation of aquatic invasive species, as defined in subdivision ten of

section 9-1703 of the environmental conservation law, in the waters of the state. The department shall provide the universal signage on its website in a downloadable format.

2. Commencing within one year of the effective date of this section, owners of each public boat launch shall conspicuously post the universal sign of not less than eighteen inches by twenty-four inches, established pursuant to subdivision one of this section, at each public boat launch in the state.

§ 36. Removal of unauthorized floating object

No unattended floating object shall be anchored within the navigable waters of the state for any purpose, except as same may be authorized under the United States laws, rules and regulations or by section thirty-five and thirty-five-a of this chapter or by local ordinances as may be duly approved by the commissioner. Any person finding such anchored object is authorized to remove the same.

§ 37. Public use of privately owned navigable waters

The provisions of this chapter shall apply to privately owned navigable waters to which the public has or is granted access, for compensation or otherwise, for boating, bathing, swimming or other recreational uses or purposes.

§ 38. Lake George water levels

Any dam or other similar structure so located in the outlet of Lake George as to affect the water levels of the lake shall, with due allowance for fluctuations due to natural causes or to emergencies and for a reasonable use of water for power and for sanitary purposes, be operated in such a manner as to maintain the waters of the lake from the first day of June to the thirtieth day of September in each year as nearly as may be at an average level of three and five-tenths feet on the gage of the United States Geological Survey at Rogers Rock on Lake George, known as Rogers Rock gage, and in such a manner as to maintain the waters of the lake from the first day of October to the first day of December at a level which shall not fall below two and five-tenths feet on said gage; and, consistent with the above mentioned fluctuations and reasonable use, the waste gates of any such dam or other structure shall be operated so that, to the extent possible, the waters of the lake will not be permitted to rise above a level of four feet on such gage at any time during the year or to fall below a level of two and five-tenths feet on said gage at any time after the first day of

June and prior to the first day of December in any year. If at any time during the year the waters of the lake shall rise above such level of four feet any person owning or operating such dam or other structure shall immediately open the waste gates thereof and take such other appropriate action as in the judgment of the water resources commission may be necessary to lower the waters of the lake with the least practicable delay to a level not higher than four feet of said gage. If at any time after the first day of June and prior to the first day of December in any year the waters of the lake shall fall below such level of two and five-tenths feet such person shall immediately close the waste gates of such dam or other structure; and no person shall withdraw water from the lake for the purpose of generating power during any period of time between the first day of June and the first day of October in any year when the level of the waters of the lake is below two and five-tenths feet on said gage. The water resources commission or its duly authorized representative shall at all times have access to such dam or other structure and is hereby authorized and directed to operate the waste gates thereof whenever necessary for the purpose of carrying out the provisions of this section. The water resources commission shall establish such rules and regulations as in its judgment may be necessary for the enforcement of the provisions of this section, and it is hereby authorized to enter into such agreement or agreements with any person or persons owning or operating any such dam or other structure as in its judgment may be necessary in order to carry into effect the provisions of this section and of such rules and regulations. In addition, the water resources commission shall, once in each year during the first week in July, cause to be published in at least three daily newspapers serving the area the reading on the Rogers Rock gage on the first day of July in that year. Any person violating any provision of this section or of any rule or regulation established or of any agreement entered into pursuant thereto shall for every such violation forfeit to the people of the state the sum of not to exceed two hundred fifty dollars to be recovered in a civil action.

§ 39. Motor boat regulation on Lake George

1. Definitions. The term "motor boat" shall be deemed to mean and include a mechanically propelled vessel having a source of power other than propulsion by wind propelled sail or human propelled oar or paddle. The term shall also include a craft temporarily or permanently equipped with a detachable motor, commonly known as an

"outboard" motor boat.

2. No motor boat shall be operated in the stream and marshland south of the Dunham's Bay highway bridge (Route 9L) south of a point which is approximately eighteen hundred feet south of the south side of the Route 9L Dunham's Bay highway bridge, at which point there will be anchored in the water two large floating buoys warning that motor boats are prohibited beyond said point.

3. No motor boat shall be operated in the stream and marshland south of the point where 9L crosses the Warner Bay inlet stream south of a point which is approximately one thousand feet south of the south side of Route 9L at the center of its crossing over the Warner Bay inlet stream at which point there will be anchored in the water two large floating buoys warning that motor boats are prohibited beyond said point.

4. No motor boat shall be operated in the stream or marshland in Harris Bay of Lake George south of Route 9L, and warning buoys shall be installed in the open water area south of Route 9L.

5. The expense attached to the purchase of the buoys, mentioned in subdivisions two, three and four of this section, which after their installation shall become part of the Lake George buoyage system, shall be payable from moneys available therefor by appropriation and from moneys, if any, contributed by persons, towns and counties interested.

6. Penalties for violations. A person violating any of the provisions of this section shall be deemed guilty of a violation and punishable by a fine of not more than fifty dollars or imprisonment for not more than ten days or by both such fine and imprisonment.

§ 39-a. Motor boat regulation on Lake Colby

1. The term "motor boat" shall mean and include a mechanically propelled vessel having a source of power in excess of ten horsepower other than propulsion by wind propelled sail or human propelled oar or paddle. Such term shall also include a vessel temporarily or permanently equipped with a detachable motor, commonly known as an "outboard" motor boat.

2. No motor boat shall be operated on Lake Colby, in the town of Harrietstown, county of Franklin.

3. The provisions of this section shall not apply to emergency and rescue vessels and

vessels operated for the official functions of a federal, state or local governmental agency.

4. A person violating any provision of subdivision two of this section shall be guilty of a violation punishable by a fine of not more than fifty dollars, or imprisonment for not more than ten days, or by both such fine and imprisonment.

Article 4 Vessels

Part 1 Vessels, General

§ 40. Equipment

Equipment required herein shall be carried on every vessel except as otherwise provided, while underway, or at anchor with any person aboard, while on the navigable waters of the state and any tidewaters bordering on or lying within the boundaries of Nassau and Suffolk counties. Should the federal government adopt vessel equipment requirements different from those contained in this section, the commissioner shall be authorized to adopt rules and regulations superceding the vessel equipment requirements of this section to achieve consistency with federal standards, and shall submit such proposed rules and regulations to the secretary of state in accordance with the state administrative procedure act within thirty days of the adoption of federal equipment requirements or submit a statement as to why such conforming changes are not being proposed.

1. Personal flotation devices.

(a) Every pleasure vessel and every rowboat, canoe and kayak shall have at least one wearable personal flotation device for each person on board, which shall be of a type approved by the United States coast guard and shall be in good condition.

(b) Pleasure vessels sixteen feet and greater in length shall carry at least one type IV throwable personal flotation device which shall be of a type approved by the United States coast guard and shall be in good condition.

(c) Every operator or person in charge or control of a pleasure vessel, rowboat or canoe, as described in paragraphs (a) and (b) of this subdivision, shall be responsible for compliance with the provisions of this subdivision.

(d) No person shall operate a pleasure vessel of Class A, one, two or three as classified and defined in subdivision one of section forty-three of this article or a rowboat, canoe or kayak nor shall the owner of such vessel while on board such vessel knowingly permit its operation, unless each person on such vessel under the age of twelve is wearing a securely fastened United States Coast Guard approved wearable personal flotation device of an appropriate size when said vessel is underway. The provisions of this paragraph shall not apply to any person on such vessel under the age of twelve who is within a fully enclosed cabin.

(e) No owner or operator of a pleasure vessel less than twenty-one feet, including rowboats, canoes, and kayaks shall permit its operation, between November first and May first, unless each person on board such vessel is wearing a securely fastened United States Coast Guard approved wearable personal flotation device of an appropriate size when such vessel is underway.

2. Whistle. Every mechanically propelled vessel shall be provided with an efficient whistle. The word "whistle" shall mean any sound producing mechanical appliance, except sirens, capable of producing a blast of two seconds or more in duration and of such strength as to be heard plainly for a distance of at least one-half mile in still weather. A siren whistle may only be attached to a vessel operated by a police department, fire department or public utility company, and used only on emergency calls. On vessels less than thirty-nine feet in length, a mouth whistle capable of producing a blast of two seconds or more in duration, which can be heard for at least one-half a mile, may be used.

3. Anchors. Every mechanically propelled vessel shall carry an anchor and cable of sufficient weight and strength to provide a safe anchorage for such vessel. It shall be the duty of the master of such vessel to exercise reasonable care and caution and maritime skill in everything relating to the safe anchorage of his vessel.

4. Carburetor backfire flame arresters. The carburetor of every gasoline engine installed in a mechanically propelled vessel after April twenty-five, nineteen hundred forty, except outboard motors, shall be fitted with a United States coast guard approved device for arresting backfire.

5. Classification of fire extinguishers. Hand portable fire extinguishers capable of extinguishing gasoline, oil or grease fires shall be classified as prescribed and approved by the commissioner.

6. Fire extinguishers required.

(a) Every mechanically propelled vessel as classified and defined by subdivision one of section forty-three of this article, except outboard motor boats less than twenty-six feet in length, of open construction, shall carry United States coast guard approved fire extinguishers in accordance with the following:

Class A motor boats shall carry one B-1 fire extinguisher.

Class 1 motor boats shall carry one B-1 fire extinguisher.

Class 2 motor boats shall carry two B-1 fire extinguishers.

Class 3 motor boats shall carry three B-1 fire extinguishers.

Class 4 motor boats shall carry fire extinguishers and other fire fighting equipment as required by the federal navigation law and rules and regulations made by the United States coast guard for uninspected vessels.

(b) One class B-2 fire extinguisher may be substituted for two class B-1 fire extinguishers.

(c) When the engine compartment of the motor boat is equipped with a fixed fire extinguishing system of a United States coast guard approved type, one less class B-1 fire extinguisher is required.

(d) No fire extinguishers of the toxic vaporizing liquid type, including those containing carbon tetrachloride and chlorobromomethane extinguishing agents shall be approved by the commissioner.

7. Visual distress signals. Every vessel of sixteen feet or more, regardless of the distance of the vessel from shore, shall carry, to be displayed and used whenever such vessel is in need of assistance, the number and type of visual distress signals that are required by the United States coast guard for operation on waters under federal jurisdiction. Such devices shall be in serviceable condition and readily accessible on board the vessel and the service life, if marked upon the device, shall not have expired. The provisions of this subdivision shall not apply to open sailboats under twenty-six feet in length that are not equipped with mechanical power or vessels participating in an organized marine event for which a permit has been granted by the commissioner pursuant to section thirty-four of this chapter, or by the United States coast guard. All vessels shall carry visual distress signals suitable for night use between sunset and sunrise. At all times the provisions of this subdivision shall not apply to vessels engaged in commerce and having a valid marine document issued by the United

States or a foreign government.

8. Ventilation. All mechanically propelled vessels, the construction or decking over of which is commenced after April twenty-fifth nineteen hundred forty, and which uses fuel having a flash point of one hundred ten degrees fahrenheit or less shall have at least two ventilators fitted with cowls or their equivalent for the purpose of properly and efficiently ventilating the bilges of every engine and fuel tank compartment in order to remove any inflammable or explosive gases. Such mechanically propelled vessels so constructed as to have the greater portion of the bilges under the engine and fuel tanks open and exposed to the natural atmosphere at all times need not be required to be fitted with such ventilators.

9. Motor boats of greater than thirty-nine feet in length shall carry a bell.

10. Any violation of the provisions of this section, or of a rule or regulation adopted pursuant to this section, shall constitute a violation punishable by a fine of not less than twenty-five nor more than one hundred dollars.

11. The provisions of this section shall not apply to vessels competing in duly authorized regattas and trials preceding such regattas.

12. Any person or business which, in the regular course of business, sells, offers for sale, leases or offers for lease new or used vessels or outboard motors to the general public shall, upon the sale or lease of any vessel or outboard motor, provide the purchaser with a list of required equipment as set forth in this section and any rule or regulation promulgated pursuant to this section.

§ 40-a. Manufacture and sale of outboard motors

No outboard motor manufactured after January first, nineteen hundred eighty shall be sold or offered for commercial sale by a dealer in this state unless such motor shall have permanently engraved thereon by the manufacturer an identifying serial number. Such serial mark shall be of a permanent nature so as to prevent or discourage the removal, defacing, alteration or destruction thereof. Anyone violating the provisions of this section shall be guilty of a violation punishable by a fine of not less than one hundred nor more than two hundred fifty dollars.

§ 40-b. Sale and use of tributyltin paint

1. No person shall sell or offer to sell quick release tributyltin antifoulant bottom paints

after January first, nineteen hundred eighty-eight. For purposes of this section, "quick release" shall mean a release rate of greater than five micrograms of tributyltin per square centimeter per day.

2. No person shall apply a quick release tributyltin antifoulant bottom paint to any vessel expected to be used in the waters of the state including the marine and coastal district, as defined in section 13-0103 of the environmental conservation law, after January first, nineteen hundred eighty-eight, nor shall any person apply an antifoulant bottom paint having a release rate of greater than one microgram or less than five micrograms of tributyltin per square centimeter per day to any non-aluminum part of any vessel less than twenty-five meters in length which is expected to be used in the waters of the state including the marine and coastal district after January first, nineteen hundred eighty-eight.

3. After January first, nineteen hundred eighty-eight, paint containers holding antifoulant bottom paint having a release rate of more than one microgram or less than five micrograms of tributyltin per square centimeter being sold or offered for retail sale shall not exceed thirty-two fluid ounces of such paint and shall have affixed to the container a label which states the application of such paint is restricted under New York state law to aluminum parts only.

4. The department of environmental conservation shall, prior to January first, nineteen hundred eighty-eight, develop a list of those quick release antifoulant bottom paints which have been banned from use in this state under the provisions of this section as well as a list of those tributyltin antifoulant bottom paints which have had their sale and application restricted under the provisions of this section. The department shall make such lists available to any interested party and shall make a reasonable effort to transmit such lists to known manufacturers and those places of sale of such paints within the state and shall until December thirty-first, nineteen hundred eighty-eight provide such list to any applicant for a license or permit under article eleven or thirteen of the environmental conservation law.

5. Any violation of this section shall be a violation punishable by a fine of not less than one hundred nor more than two hundred fifty dollars.

§ 41. Pilot rules

The following rules shall be observed on all mechanically propelled vessels on the navigable waters of the state and all tidewaters bordering on or lying within the boundaries of Nassau and Suffolk counties:

1. Signals. The signals for passing, by the blowing of the whistle, shall at all times be given by the master as defined in this act.

(a) One distinct blast of the whistle shall mean: "I direct my course to starboard"; except when two vessels are approaching each other at right angles or obliquely, when it shall signify the intention of the vessel which is to starboard of the other to hold course and speed.

(b) Two distinct blasts of the whistle shall mean: "I direct my course to port."

(c) Three distinct blasts of the whistle shall mean: "My engines are going at full speed astern."

(d) Four distinct blasts of the whistle shall mean: "I am in distress and need your assistance."

(e) Five or more distinct blasts of the whistle shall constitute the "danger signal."

(f) It shall be forbidden to use what has become technically known among pilots as "cross-signals"; that is answering one whistle with two, or two whistles with one.

(g) When a vessel is under way in a fog, mist, falling snow, or heavy rain storm, it shall be the duty of the master to cause a long blast of the whistle to be sounded at intervals not exceeding one minute. When towing other vessels the long blast of the whistle shall be followed by two short blasts. Such vessel shall proceed at a moderate speed and with caution, having careful regard to the existing circumstances and conditions.

(h) The master of a vessel, when at anchor during a fog, mist, falling snow or heavy rain storm, shall, at intervals of not more than one minute, ring a bell rapidly or sound other warning signals for about five seconds.

2. Positions.

(a) When vessels are approaching each other "head and head," that is, end on or nearly so, it shall be the duty of each to pass on the port side of the other, and either vessel shall give, as a signal of her intention, one distinct blast on her whistle, which the other vessel shall answer promptly with one similar blast of her whistle.

(b) When vessels are approaching each other and the courses of such vessels are so far to the starboard of each other as not to be considered to be meeting head on or nearly so, either vessel shall immediately give two distinct blasts of her whistle, which the other shall answer promptly with two similar blasts of her whistle, and they shall pass on the starboard side of each other.

(c) When vessels are approaching each other at "right angles or obliquely" so as to involve risk of collision, the vessel which has the other on her own port side shall hold her course and speed, and shall so signify with one distinct blast of her whistle; and the vessel which has the other on her own starboard side shall keep out of the way of the other by directing her course to starboard so as to cross the stern of the other vessel, or, if necessary to do so, shall slacken her speed, or stop or reverse.

(d) When vessels are running in the same direction and the vessel which is astern shall desire to pass on the starboard side of the vessel ahead, she shall give one distinct blast of her whistle as the signal of such desire, and if the vessel ahead answers with one similar blast of her whistle, she shall pass to the starboard; or if the vessel astern shall desire to pass on the port side of the vessel ahead, she shall give two distinct blasts of her whistle as a signal of such desire, and, if the vessel ahead answers with two similar blasts of the whistle, she shall pass to the port; but if the vessel ahead does not think it safe for the vessel astern to pass at that point, she shall immediately signify the same by giving five or more rapid blasts of her whistle (the danger signal), and under no circumstances shall the vessel astern attempt to pass the vessel ahead until such time as they have reached a point where it can be safely done, when said vessel ahead shall signify her willingness by blowing the proper signal, which shall be answered by the vessel astern. Neither vessel shall in any case attempt to cross the bow or to crowd upon the course of the other vessel.

(e) If when vessels are approaching each other head and head, that is, end on or nearly so, (as per subdivision (a) and (b)) or crossing each other's courses, (as per subdivision (c)), or desire to pass each other (as per subdivision (d)), either vessel fails to understand the course or intention of the other, from any cause, the vessel so in doubt shall immediately signify the same by giving five or more rapid blasts of her whistle, (the danger signal), and both vessels shall immediately slow their speed, or stop or reverse, as required to avoid collision, until proper signals have been given, answered and understood, or until the vessels have passed each other.

(f) When a mechanically propelled vessel shall meet a sailing vessel proceeding in such direction as to involve risk of collision, the sailing vessel shall have the right of way. It shall be incumbent on the master of the sailing vessel to keep a vigilant lookout and change her course, if necessary, to avoid any danger.

(g) In narrow channels, every vessel shall, when it is safe and practicable, keep to that side of the fairway or mid-channel which lies on the starboard side of such vessel.

3. Aid in distress. It shall be the duty of every master or pilot of any vessel to render such assistance as he can possibly give to any other vessel coming under his observation and being in distress on account of accident, collision or otherwise.

4. Construing rules. In obeying and construing these rules, due regard shall be had to all dangers of navigation and collision, and to any special circumstances which may render a departure from the above rules necessary in order to avoid immediate danger.

5. Application. The rules of this section shall apply to all vessels, public and pleasure, propelled by machinery on the navigable waters of the state and all tidewaters bordering on or lying within the boundaries of Nassau and Suffolk counties.

6. Commissioner may modify. The commissioner is hereby authorized to modify, change or expand the pilot rules as set forth in this section if necessary to make them comply or be uniform with the provisions of the federal navigation law, or of the navigation rules and regulations made by the United States coast guard.

7. A violation of any provision of this section shall constitute a violation punishable as set forth in section seventy-three-c of this article.

§ 42. Searchlights; unlawful to flash

Any licensed master, pilot, joint pilot and engineer or operator, who shall flash or cause to be flashed, the rays of a searchlight into the pilot house or into the eyes of the master, pilot, or operator of an approaching vessel shall be liable to have his license revoked. Any person committing such act shall be guilty of a misdemeanor punishable as set forth in section seventy-three-b of this article. Searchlights shall not be known as navigating lights.

§ 42-a. Tow-chains

Any person, for a fee, who operates a boat or vessel, and who pilots, offers to pilot, tows or offers to tow any other boat or vessel, must remove completely from the water any rope or chain or other tool or device used to connect the boats or vessels for the purposes of towing, while such rope or chain or other tool or device is not being used to tow another boat or vessel. Violation of this section is a violation, punishable by a fine of not less than two hundred fifty dollars and not more than one thousand dollars.

§ 43. Lights to be displayed

1. Vessels classified. For the application of this section vessels shall be divided into classes as follows:

Class A. Less than sixteen feet in length.

Class 1. Sixteen feet or over and less than twenty-six feet in length.

Class 2. Twenty-six feet or over and less than forty feet in length.

Class 3. Forty feet or over and not more than sixty-five feet in length.

Class 4. Over sixty-five feet in length.

Class 5. Rowboats, canoes and kayaks.

2. Every vessel in all weathers from sunset to sunrise shall carry and exhibit and, if carried, shall also exhibit from sunrise to sunset in restricted visibility, and may exhibit in all other circumstances when it is deemed necessary, the following lights when under way, and during such times no other lights which may be mistaken for those prescribed shall be exhibited:

(a) Every vessel of classes A and one shall carry the following lights:

First. A bright white light aft to show all around the horizon.

Second. A combined lantern in the fore part of the vessel and lower than the white light aft, showing green to starboard and red to port, so fixed as to throw the light from right ahead to two points abaft the beam on their respective sides.

(b) Every vessel of classes two and three shall carry the following lights:

First. A bright white light in the fore part of the vessel as near the stem as practicable, so constructed as to show an unbroken light over an arc of the horizon of twenty points of the compass, so fixed as to throw the light ten points on each side of the vessel; namely, from right ahead to two points abaft the beam on either side.

Second. A bright white light aft to show all around the horizon and higher than the white light forward.

Third. On the starboard side a green light so constructed as to show an unbroken light over an arc of the horizon of ten points of the compass, so fixed as to throw the light from right ahead to two points abaft the beam on the starboard side. On the port side a red light so constructed as to show an unbroken light over an arc of the horizon of ten points of the compass, so fixed as to throw the light from right ahead to two points abaft the beam on the port side. The said side lights shall be fitted with inboard screens of sufficient height so set as to prevent these lights from being seen across the bow.

(c) Every vessel of class four shall carry the following lights:

First. On or in front of the foremast, or, if a vessel without a foremast, then in the fore part of the vessel, a bright white light so constructed as to show an unbroken light over an arc of the horizon of twenty points of the compass, so fixed as to throw light ten points on each side of the vessel, namely from right ahead to two points abaft the beam on either side, and of such character as to be visible at a distance of at least five miles.

Second. An additional after white light carried at an elevation at least fifteen feet above the light at the head of the vessel and to show all around the horizon.

Third. On the starboard side a green light so constructed as to show an unbroken light over an arc of the horizon of ten points of the compass, so fixed as to throw the light from right ahead to two points abaft the beam on the starboard side. On the port side a red light so constructed as to show an unbroken light over an arc of the horizon of ten points of the compass, so fixed as to throw the light from right ahead to two points abaft the beam on the port side. The said side lights shall be fitted with inboard screens of sufficient height so set as to prevent these lights from being seen across the bow.

(d) Rowboats, canoes and kayaks, whether under oars or sail, shall have ready at hand a lantern showing a white light which shall be temporarily exhibited in sufficient time to prevent collision.

(e) Vessels of classes A and one when propelled by sail alone shall carry the combined lantern, but not the white light aft, prescribed by this section. Vessels of classes two and three, when so propelled, shall carry the colored side lights, suitably screened, but not the white lights, prescribed by this section. Vessels of all classes, when so propelled, shall carry, ready at hand, a lantern or flashlight showing a white light which shall be exhibited in sufficient time to avert collision.

(f) When propelled by sail and machinery any vessel shall carry the lights required by this section for a vessel propelled by machinery only.

(g) Any vessel may carry and exhibit the lights required by the federal regulations for preventing collisions at sea, nineteen hundred forty-eight, act of October eleventh, nineteen hundred fifty-one, as amended, in lieu of the lights required by this section.

(h) A mechanically propelled vessel when towing another vessel shall, in addition to her side lights, carry two bright white lights in a vertical line one over the other, not less than three feet apart.

(i) A vessel under one hundred fifty feet in length when at anchor shall carry forward, where it can best be seen, but at a height not exceeding twenty feet above the hull, a white light in a lantern so constructed as to show a clear, uniform, and unbroken light visible all around the horizon at a distance of at least one mile: provided that the commissioner may, after investigation, by rule, regulation, or order, designate such areas as he may deem proper as "special anchorage areas"; such special anchorage areas may from time to time be changed, or abolished, if after investigation the commissioner shall deem such change or abolishment in the interest of navigation: provided further that vessels not more than sixty-five feet in length when at anchor in any such special anchorage area shall not be required to carry or exhibit the white light required by this subdivision. A vessel of one hundred fifty feet or upward in length, when at anchor, shall carry in the forward part of the vessel, at a height of not less than twenty feet and not exceeding forty feet above the hull, one such light, and at or near the stern of the vessel, and at such a height that it shall be not less than fifteen feet lower than the forward light, another such light.

(j) Every white light prescribed by this section shall be of such character as to be visible at a distance of at least two miles except as otherwise provided. Every colored light prescribed by this section shall be of such character as to be visible at a distance of at least one mile except as otherwise provided. The word "visible" in this section when applied to lights, shall mean visible on a dark night with clear atmosphere.

(k) A revolving blue light may only be carried or exhibited on enforcement vessels owned or operated by the state of New York or a political subdivision thereof.

(l) For the purposes of this section, the term "restricted visibility" shall mean any condition in which visibility is restricted by fog, mist, falling snow, heavy rainstorms, sandstorms, or any other similar causes;

3. Should the federal government adopt vessel light requirements different from those contained in this section, the commissioner shall be authorized to adopt rules and regulations superseding the vessel light requirements of this section to achieve consistency with federal standards, and shall submit such proposed rules and regulations to the secretary of state in accordance with the state administrative procedure act within thirty days of the adoption of federal equipment requirements or submit a statement as to why such conforming changes are not being proposed.

4. A violation of any provision of this section, or of a rule or regulation adopted pursuant to subdivision three of this section, shall constitute a violation punishable by a fine of not less than twenty-five nor more than one hundred dollars.

§ 44. Noise levels on pleasure vessels

1. The provisions of this section shall apply to the navigable waters of the state including all tidewaters bordering on and lying within the boundaries of Nassau and Suffolk counties.

2.

(a) No person shall operate or give permission for the operation of any pleasure vessel in or upon the waters of this state in such a manner as to exceed a noise level of 90dB(A) when subjected to a stationary sound level test as prescribed by SAE J 2005.

(b) No person shall operate a pleasure vessel on the waters of this state in such a manner as to exceed a noise level of 75dB(A) measured as specified in SAE J 1970. Provided, that such measurement shall not preclude a stationary sound level test as prescribed by SAE J 2005.

3. Sale or manufacture. No person shall manufacture or offer for sale any pleasure vessel or engine for use in a pleasure vessel for use on the waters of this state if such vessel or engine, at the time of manufacture or sale, cannot be operated in such a manner so as to comply with the sound level requirements provided in this section.

4. No person shall operate or give permission for the operation of any pleasure vessel in or upon the waters of this state that is equipped with an altered muffler or a muffler cutout, bypass or otherwise reduce or eliminate the effectiveness of any muffler or muffler system

installed in accordance with this section.

5. No person shall remove, alter or otherwise modify in any way a muffler or muffler system in a manner which will prevent it from being operated in accordance with this section.

6. Exceptions. The provisions of this section shall not apply to pleasure vessels designed, manufactured and sold for the sole purpose of competing in racing events and for no other purpose. Any such exemption or exception shall be so documented in any and every sale agreement and shall be formally acknowledged by signature on the part of both the buyer and the seller and copies of said agreement shall be maintained by both parties. A copy shall be kept on board whenever the pleasure vessel is operated. Any pleasure vessel sold under this exemption may only be operated on the waters of this state in accordance with this section. The provisions of this section shall also not apply to:

(a) Pleasure vessels which are competing in or participating for a definite race over a given course held under the auspices of any bona fide club or racing association between the hours of nine o' clock in the morning and sunset, which has been approved pursuant to the provisions of section thirty-four of this chapter, and all provisions of such section have been complied with or pursuant to authorization by the commandant of the United States Coast Guard.

(b) An authorized agent of the federal, state or municipal government when operating a pleasure vessel necessary to carry out his or her official duty of enforcement, search and rescue, firefighting or research programs.

(c) A pleasure vessel being operated by a boat or marine engine manufacturer for the purposes of testing and/or development.

(d) A pleasure vessel manufactured prior to nineteen hundred sixty-five.

7. Any officer authorized to enforce the provisions of this section who has reason to believe that a pleasure vessel is not in compliance with the noise levels established in this section may direct the operator of such pleasure vessel to submit the pleasure vessel to an on-site test to measure noise level, with the officer on board if such officer chooses, and the operator shall comply with such request. If such pleasure vessel exceeds the decibel levels established in this section, the officer may direct the operator to take immediate and reasonable measures to correct the violation, including returning the pleasure vessel to a mooring and

keeping the pleasure vessel at such mooring until the violation is corrected or ceases.

8. Any officer who conducts pleasure vessel sound level tests as provided in this section shall be qualified in pleasure vessel noise testing by the department of parks, recreation and historic preservation. Such qualifications shall include but may not be limited to the selection of the measurement site, and the calibration and use of noise testing equipment.

9. Penalties.

(a) Any person who fails to comply with the provisions of this section shall be guilty of a violation punishable by a fine not to exceed fifty dollars for the first offense and not exceeding two hundred fifty dollars for a second or subsequent offense. However, the court shall waive any fine for which a person who violates the provisions of this section would be liable if such person supplies the court with proof within thirty days of the issuance of the summons that he purchased his pleasure vessel prior to the effective date of this section, that the pleasure vessel's muffler was not altered or made inoperable so as to result in a violation of the provisions of this section, and that the pleasure vessel has been repaired, altered or modified so as to be in compliance with the provisions of this section. Provided, however, that such waiver of fine shall not apply to a second or subsequent conviction under this section.

(b) Any person who alters or makes inoperable an effective muffler system so that such system is no longer in compliance with this section shall be guilty of a violation punishable by a fine of not less than fifty dollars nor more than two hundred fifty dollars.

(c) All fines and forfeitures collected pursuant to the provisions of this section by any court, judge, magistrate or other officer referred to in subdivision one of section thirty-nine of the judiciary law, establishing a unified court budget, shall be paid to the state commissioner of taxation and finance, within the first ten days of the month following collection to be deposited in a fund known as the boating noise level enforcement fund established pursuant to section ninety-one-b of the state finance law. The office of parks, recreation and historic preservation shall distribute the fines to local law enforcement officials according to the provisions of section seventy-nine-b of this chapter for the purpose of enforcing the provisions of this section.

10. All fines and forfeitures collected by any other court, judge or magistrate or other

officer shall be paid to the state comptroller within the first ten days of the month following collection to be deposited in a fund known as the boating noise level enforcement fund established pursuant to section ninety-one-b of the state finance law. The office of parks, recreation and historic preservation shall distribute the fines to local law enforcement officials according to the provisions of section seventy-nine-b of this chapter for the purpose of enforcing the provisions of this section.

§ 44-a. [Repealed]

§ 44-b. [Repealed]

§ 44-c. [Repealed]

§ 44-d. [Repealed]

§ 44-e. [Repealed]

§ 45. Reckless operation of a vessel; speed

1.

(a)   Every master or operator of a vessel shall at all times navigate the same in a careful and prudent manner in such a way as not to unreasonably interfere with the free and proper use of the navigable waters of the state and all tidewaters bordering on or lying within the boundaries of Nassau and Suffolk counties or unreasonably endanger any vessel or person. Reckless operation is prohibited. Any person operating a vessel in violation of this subdivision shall be guilty of a misdemeanor punishable as set forth in section seventy-three-b of this article.

(b)   No person shall operate a vessel at a speed greater than is reasonable and prudent under the conditions and having regard to the actual and potential hazards then existing.

1-a.   No vessel other than the tending vessel shall be operated within one hundred feet of a red flag with a diagonal white bar which, when displayed on the water or from a boat, indicates underwater diving, or a designated course for racing shells but no such flag shall be placed so as to deny access or use of any boathouse, wharf, harbor, bay, channel or navigable waterway.

2.   Except as provided in section forty-five-cc of this part, no vessel shall be operated within one hundred feet of the shore, a dock, pier, raft, float or an anchored or moored vessel at a speed exceeding five miles per hour, unless such vessel is being operated near such shore,

dock, float, pier, raft, or anchored vessel for the purpose of enabling a person engaged in water skiing to take off or land.

3. The provisions of this section shall not apply to a vessel while actually competing in a regatta or boat race authorized under section thirty-four of this chapter.

4. The provisions of subdivision two above shall not apply to commercial vessels having a valid marine document issued by the United States or a foreign government.

5. The violation of any of the provisions of this section other than paragraph (a) of subdivision one of this section shall constitute a violation punishable as set forth in section seventy-three-c of this article.

6. [None]

7.

(a) The court may suspend a person's privilege to operate a vessel for a period of at least three but less than twelve months upon conviction for reckless operation of a vessel pursuant to any applicable provision of this article. In determining the length of such suspension, the court may take into consideration the seriousness of the offense and may impose a period of suspension whereby such suspension may be in effect during a portion of the current or subsequent boating season.

(b) The court shall suspend a person's privilege to operate and may suspend a vessel registration:

(1) for a period of at least six but less than twelve months where a person is convicted of reckless operation of a vessel pursuant to any applicable provision of this article after having been convicted of any such offense within the preceding eighteen months. In determining the length of such suspension or suspensions, the court may take into consideration the seriousness of the offense and may impose a period of suspension whereby such suspension may be in effect during a portion of the current or subsequent boating season;

(2) for a period of at least six but less than twelve months upon a third or subsequent conviction for any violation of any law, ordinance or regulation limiting the speed of a vessel or any provision constituted a misdemeanor by this article except for the commission of a third or subsequent misdemeanor as set forth in subparagraph three of this paragraph. In determining the length of such suspension or suspensions, the court may take into

consideration the seriousness of the offense and may impose a period of suspension whereby such suspension may be in effect during a portion of the current or subsequent boating season;

(3) for a period of twelve months where a person is convicted of reckless operation of a vessel pursuant to any applicable provision of this article after having been twice convicted of any such offense within the preceding eighteen months.

(c) When a person is convicted pursuant to this article the court may, in any case before the court, and shall when the convicted person is subject to a suspension pursuant to this subdivision, in addition to any other penalties invoked under this article, require the convicted person, as a condition of the sentence, to complete a boating safety course of the state, U.S. Power Squadrons, U.S. Coast Guard Auxiliary, or a powerboating course or courses offered by the United States sailing association which are approved by the commissioner and show proof of successful completion of such course to the court or its designee.

§ 45-a. Beaching a disabled water craft

Except in an emergency, it shall not be lawful to intentionally beach or abandon any vessel, ship, boat or other water craft on underwater lands of navigable waters of the state surrounding Richmond county, without the permission of the owners or lessees of the uplands abutting such underwater lands. Any violation of this section shall be a misdemeanor punishable as set forth in section seventy-three-b of this article.

§ 45-aa. Special provisions relating to reckless operation and speed on Canandaigua lake; Keuka lake

1. Notwithstanding any other provisions of this chapter or any inconsistent local laws (a) every pleasure vessel operated on Canandaigua lake, which is bordered by Ontario and Yates counties, shall be operated in a careful and prudent manner, in such a way as not to unreasonably interfere with or endanger any other vessel or person; a violation of this paragraph shall be a misdemeanor punishable as set forth in section seventy-three-b of this article; and (b) no vessel shall be operated on such lake at a speed exceeding forty-five miles per hour nor shall any pleasure vessel be operated at a speed exceeding twenty-five miles per hour between one-half hour after sunset and one-half hour before sunrise; a violation of this paragraph shall be a violation punishable as set forth in section seventy-three-c of

this article.

1-a. Notwithstanding any other provisions of this chapter or any inconsistent local laws (a) every vessel operated on Keuka Lake, which is bordered by Steuben and Yates counties, shall be operated in a careful and prudent manner, in such a way as not to unreasonably interfere with or endanger any other vessel or person; a violation of this paragraph shall be a misdemeanor punishable as set forth in section seventy-three-b of this article; and (b) no vessel shall be operated on such lake at a speed exceeding forty-five miles per hour nor shall any vessel be operated at a speed exceeding twenty-five miles per hour between one-half hour after sunset and one-half hour before sunrise; a violation of this paragraph shall be a violation punishable as set forth in section seventy-three-c of this article.

2. No vessel shall be operated within two hundred feet of the shore, a dock, pier, raft or float or an anchored or moored vessel at a speed exceeding five miles per hour, unless such vessel is being operated near such shore, dock, float, pier, raft or anchored vessel for the purpose of enabling a person engaged in water skiing to take off or land. A violation of this subdivision shall be a violation punishable as set forth in section seventy-three-c of this article.

3. The provisions of this section shall not apply to any pleasure vessel competing in or practicing for a regatta or boat race over a specified course held by a bona fide club or racing association between nine o' clock in the morning and sunset, provided that due written notice of the date of the race has been given to the appropriate law enforcement agency at least fifteen days prior to such race, pursuant to the provisions of section thirty-four of this chapter, and all provisions of this section have been complied with.

4. Nothing in this section shall be construed as prohibiting any city, town or village from continuing, adopting or enacting any other local laws relating to persons operating a pleasure vessel within its limits, but no such municipality shall have the power to make less restrictive any of such provisions.

§ 45-aaa. Special provisions relating to speed on Irondequoit bay

1. No vessel shall be operated on Irondequoit bay, which is located within Monroe county, at a speed exceeding twenty-five miles per hour unless such vessel is being operated for the purpose of enabling a person engaged in water skiing or other water sport to be towed,

in which case no such vessel shall be operated at a speed exceeding thirty-five miles per hour.

2. No vessel shall be operated in the channel between Irondequoit Bay and Lake Ontario or within three hundred feet of the shore, the channel, a dock, pier, raft or float or an anchored or moored vessel in a manner or at a speed that causes a wake that unreasonably interferes with or endangers such dock, pier, raft or float or an anchored or moored vessel but in no event at a speed exceeding five miles per hour, unless for the purpose of enabling a person engaged in water skiing to take off or land.

3. The provisions of this section shall not apply to any vessel competing in or practicing for a regatta or boat race over a specified course held by a bona fide club or racing association, provided that due written notice of the date of the race has been given to the appropriate law enforcement agency at least fifteen days prior to such race, pursuant to the provisions of section thirty-four of this chapter, and all provisions of this section have been complied with.

4. Any person who operates a vessel in violation of any of the provisions of this section shall be guilty of a violation punishable as set forth in section seventy-three-c of this article.

5. Nothing in this section shall be construed as prohibiting any town or county from continuing, adopting or enacting any other local laws, resolutions or ordinances related to persons operating a vessel within its limits, but no such municipality shall have the power to make less restrictive any of such provisions.

*§ 45-aaaa. Special provisions relating to reckless operation and speed on Greenwood Lake

1. Notwithstanding any other provisions of this chapter or any inconsistent local laws (a) every pleasure vessel operated on Greenwood Lake within Orange county, shall be operated in a careful and prudent manner, in such a way as not to unreasonably interfere with or endanger any other vessel or person; a violation of this paragraph shall be a misdemeanor punishable as set forth in section seventy-three-b of this article; and (b) no vessel shall be operated on such lake at a speed exceeding forty-five miles per hour nor shall any pleasure vessel be operated at a speed exceeding fifteen miles per hour between one-half hour after sunset and one-half hour before sunrise; a violation of this paragraph shall be a violation punishable as set forth in section seventy-three-c of this article.

2. No vessel shall be operated within two hundred feet of the shore, a dock, pier, raft or float or an anchored or moored vessel at a speed exceeding five miles per hour, unless such vessel is being operated near such shore, dock, float, pier, raft or anchored vessel for the purpose of enabling a person engaged in water skiing to take off or land. A violation of this subdivision shall be a violation punishable as set forth in section seventy-three-c of this article.

3. The provisions of this section shall not apply to any pleasure vessel competing in or practicing for a regatta or boat race over a specified course held by a bona fide club or racing association between nine o' clock in the morning and sunset, provided that due written notice of the date of the race has been given to the appropriate law enforcement agency at least fifteen days prior to such race, pursuant to the provisions of section thirty-four of this chapter, and all provisions of this section have been complied with.

*§ 45-aaaa. Special provisions relating to speed on Sodus Bay

1. No vessel shall be operated within that area of the Sodus Bay Channel and Sodus Bay bounded and described as follows: Beginning at the Sodus outer light at the north-westerly most point of the west breakwall of the Sodus Bay Channel and running thence southerly to the south-west corner of such breakwall; thence running south-westerly along the shoreline of Sodus Point; thence south-easterly along the shoreline of Sand Point to the easterly most point on said Sand Point, said point being more specifically defined as latitude 431558 [43°15'58"]*, longitude 765814 [76°58'14"]**; thence northerly across Sodus Bay to a point on the east breakwall, said point more specifically being defined as latitude 43°16'4", longitude 76°58'3"; thence westerly along said breakwall to the south-west corner and then northerly along the east pier to the east pier light on the Sodus Bay Channel; thence north-westerly to the point in place of beginning in a manner or at a speed that causes a wake that unreasonably interferes with or endangers a dock, pier, raft, float, anchored or moored vessel or swimmer but in no event at a speed exceeding five miles per hour.

2. For the purpose of complying with the provisions of this section, the sheriff of the county of Wayne is directed to place buoy markers on that portion of Sodus Bay between the easterly most point of Sand Point and the point on east breakwall which is the termination of the zone established above for the purpose of advising users of the bay of the existence

of the limited speed zone established herein.

3. Any person who operates a vessel in violation of any of the provisions of this section shall be guilty of a violation punishable as set forth in section seventy-three-c of this article.

4. Nothing in this section shall be construed as prohibiting any town or county from adopting or enacting any local laws, resolutions or ordinances related to persons operating a vessel within its limits, but no such municipality shall have the power to make less restrictive any of such provisions.

§ 45-aaaaa. Special provisions relating to reckless operation and speed on Lake Alice

1. Notwithstanding any other provisions of this chapter or any inconsistent local laws (a) every pleasure vessel operated on Lake Alice within Orleans county, shall be operated in a careful and prudent manner, in such a way as not to unreasonably interfere with or endanger any other vessel or person; a violation of this paragraph is a misdemeanor punishable as set forth in section seventy-three-b of this article; and (b) no vessel shall be operated on such lake at a speed exceeding thirty-five miles per hour; a violation of this paragraph shall be a violation punishable as set forth in section seventy-three-c of this article.

2. No vessel shall be operated within one hundred feet of the shore, a dock, pier, raft or float or an anchored or moored vessel at a speed exceeding five miles per hour, unless such vessel is being operated near such shore, dock, float, pier, raft or anchored vessel for the purpose of enabling a person engaged in water skiing to take off or land. A violation of this subdivision shall be a violation punishable as set forth in section seventy-three-c of this article.

3. The provisions of this section shall not apply to any pleasure vessel competing in or practicing for a regatta or boat race over a specified course held by a bona fide club or racing association between nine o' clock in the morning and sunset, provided that due written notice of the date of the race has been given to the appropriate law enforcement agency at least fifteen days prior to such race, pursuant to the provisions of section thirty-four of this chapter, and all provisions of such section thirty-four have been complied with.

*§ 45-aaaaaa. Special provisions relating to noise and speed on Lamoka Lake and Waneta Lake

1. Notwithstanding any other provisions of this chapter or any inconsistent local laws, every

pleasure vessel operated on Lamoka Lake, located in Schuyler county, or Waneta Lake, located in Schuyler and Steuben counties, shall be operated in a careful and prudent manner, in such a way as not to unreasonably interfere with or endanger any vessel or person, and no vessel shall be operated at a speed exceeding forty-five miles per hour. No pleasure vessel operated on Lamoka Lake or Waneta Lake shall be operated at a speed exceeding twenty-five miles per hour between one-half hour after sunset and one-half hour before sunrise.

2. No vessel shall be operated on Lamoka Lake or Waneta Lake within two hundred feet of the shore, a dock, pier, raft or float or an anchored or moored vessel in a manner or at such a speed that causes a wake that unreasonably interferes with or endangers such dock, pier, raft or float or an anchored or moored vessel but in no event at a speed exceeding five miles per hour, unless for the purpose of enabling a person engaged in water skiing to take off or land or such vessel is required to run at full throttle through an established course to measure the vessel's decibel level pursuant to the directions of a law enforcement officer.

3. The provisions of this section shall not apply to any vessel competing in or practicing for a regatta or boat race over a specified course held by a bona fide club or racing association, provided that due written notice of the date of the race has been given to the appropriate law enforcement agencies at least fifteen days prior to such race, pursuant to the provisions of section thirty-four of this chapter, and all provisions of this section have been complied with. The provisions of this section shall not apply to any Federal Aviation Agency licensed aircraft.

4. Any person who fails to comply with any of the provisions of this section shall be guilty of a violation punishable by a fine of not less than twenty-five dollars nor more than one hundred dollars for the first offense; by a fine of not less than fifty dollars nor more than two hundred dollars for conviction of the second offense committed within a period of twenty-four months; by a fine of not less than one hundred dollars nor more than two hundred dollars for conviction of the third offense or any subsequent offense committed within a period of twenty-four months.

*§ 45-aaaaaa. Special provisions relating to reckless operation, noise and speed on the Fulton Chain of Lakes

1. Notwithstanding any other provisions of this chapter or any inconsistent local laws (a) every pleasure vessel operated on the Fulton Chain of Lakes, consisting of Old Forge Pond and First through Eighth Lakes, shall be operated in a careful and prudent manner, in such a way as not to unreasonably interfere with or endanger any vessel or person; a violation of this paragraph shall be a misdemeanor punishable as set forth in section seventy-three-b of this article; and (b) no vessel shall be operated on such lake at a speed exceeding forty-five miles per hour nor shall any pleasure vessel be operated at a speed exceeding twenty-five miles per hour between one-half hour after sunset and one-half hour before sunrise; a violation of this paragraph shall be a violation punishable as set forth in section seventy-three-c of this article.

2. Except for Sixth and Seventh Lakes, no vessel shall be operated on the Fulton Chain of Lakes within two hundred feet of the shore, a dock, pier, raft or float or an anchored or moored vessel in a manner or at such a speed that causes a wake that unreasonably interferes with or endangers such dock, pier, raft or float or an anchored or moored vessel but in no event at a speed exceeding five miles per hour, unless for the purpose of enabling a person engaged in water skiing to take off or land or such vessel is required to run at full throttle through an established course to measure the vessel's decibel level pursuant to the directions of a law enforcement officer. A violation of this subdivision shall be a violation punishable as set forth in section seventy-three-c of this article.

3. Notwithstanding any other provision of this chapter or any inconsistent local laws, no person shall operate any pleasure vessel, upon the waters of the Fulton Chain of Lakes that exceeds the following noise levels: (a) for engines manufactured before September first, nineteen hundred eighty-nine, a noise level of eighty-six dbl.; (b) for engines manufactured on or after September first, nineteen hundred eighty-nine and before September first, nineteen hundred ninety-one, a noise level of eighty-four dbl.; (c) and for engines manufactured after September first, nineteen hundred ninety-one, a noise level of eighty-two dbl. All decibel levels are to be measured on a decibel meter gauged to an A-weighted scale. A violation of this subdivision shall be a violation punishable as set forth in section

seventy-three-c of this article.

4. Any law enforcement officer from the state of New York, Herkimer or Hamilton county, or any political subdivision of those counties, may direct the operator of any pleasure vessel reasonably believed to be exceeding the allowable noise levels on the Fulton Chain of Lakes to an area established by the officer for measuring vessel noise levels. At that area the vessel shall be operated at full throttle through a straight course not to exceed one hundred yards. Decibel measurements shall be measured at a distance of at least fifty feet from the pleasure vessel being tested while such vessel is at full throttle.

5. The provisions of this section shall not apply to any vessel competing in or practicing for a regatta or boat race over a specified course held by a bona fide club or racing association, provided that due written notice of the date of the race has been given to the appropriate law enforcement agencies at least fifteen days prior to such race, pursuant to the provisions of section thirty-four of this chapter, and all provisions of such section have been complied with. The provisions of this section shall not apply to any Federal Aviation Agency licensed aircraft.

§ 45-b. Regulation of beaches

Except when prohibited by reason of the laws of the United States, the board of trustees of a village may adopt, amend and enforce rules and regulations not inconsistent with law, with respect to regulating the use of beaches in or adjacent to the village and regulating swimming and bathing in open waters exposed to the public, including the use of underwater diving devices for swimming and fishing, within or bounding the village or such beaches to a distance of fifteen hundred feet from the shore, including any waters within or bordering a village in the county of Nassau or Suffolk, and requiring the owners or operators of any bathing beaches, bath houses or other places charging a fee to the public for the use of such facilities to provide adequate safeguards for the protection of the public in waters adjacent to such premises.

The provisions of this section shall be controlling notwithstanding any contrary provisions of law.

§ 45-c. Special provisions relating to reckless operation and speed on Conesus lake

1. Notwithstanding any other provisions of this chapter or any inconsistent local laws (a)

every pleasure vessel operated on Conesus lake within the county of Livingston, shall be operated in a careful and prudent manner, in such a way as not to unreasonably interfere with or endanger any other vessel or person; a violation of this paragraph shall be a misdemeanor punishable as set forth in section seventy-three-b of this article; and (b) no vessel shall be operated on such lake at a speed exceeding forty-five miles per hour nor shall any pleasure vessel be operated at a speed exceeding twenty-five miles per hour between one-half hour after sunset and one-half hour before sunrise; a violation of this paragraph shall be a violation punishable as set forth in section seventy-three-c of this article.

2. No vessel shall be operated within two hundred feet of the shore, a dock, pier, raft or float or an anchored or moored vessel at a speed exceeding five miles per hour, unless such vessel is being operated near such shore, dock, float, pier, raft or anchored vessel for the purpose of enabling a person engaged in water skiing to take off or land. A violation of this subdivision shall be a violation punishable as set forth in section seventy-three-c of this article.

3. The provisions of this section shall not apply to any pleasure vessel competing in or practicing for a regatta or boat race over a specified course held by a bona fide club or racing association between nine o' clock in the morning and sunset, provided that due written notice of the date of the race has been given to the appropriate law enforcement agency at least fifteen days prior to such race, pursuant to the provisions of section thirty-four of this chapter, and all provisions of such section have been complied with.

§ 45-cc. Reckless operation and speed on the canal system

1. Notwithstanding any other provisions of this chapter or any inconsistent local laws, every vessel operated on the canal system, as defined in subdivision one of section two of the canal law, shall be operated in a careful and prudent manner in such a way as not to unreasonably interfere with or endanger any other vessel or person. A violation of this subdivision or any applicable rules and regulations shall be a misdemeanor punishable as set forth in section seventy-three-b of this article.

2. Notwithstanding any other provisions of this chapter or any inconsistent local laws, no vessel shall be operated on such canal system within one hundred feet of the shore, a dock,

pier, raft, float or an anchored or moored vessel at a speed exceeding five miles per hour, unless such vessel is being operated near such shore, dock, float, pier, raft, or anchored vessel for the purpose of enabling a person engaged in water skiing to take off or land, and except in those areas where the canal corporation has established a different speed by rule and regulation pursuant to the canal law. A violation of this subdivision or any applicable rules and regulations shall be a violation punishable as set forth in section seventy-three-c of this article.

§ 45-d. Special provisions relating to speed at Crooke's Point in Great Kills Harbor

1. No vessel shall be operated in Great Kills Harbor extending beyond the Crooke's Point Jetty to the lighted buoy at the Harbor's entrance, within one hundred feet of the shore, a dock, pier, raft or float or an anchored or moored vessel in a manner or at a speed that causes a wake that unreasonably interferes with or endangers such dock, pier, raft or float or an anchored or moored vessel but in no event at a speed exceeding five miles per hour, unless for the purpose of enabling a person engaged in water skiing to take off or land.

2. The provisions of this section shall not apply to any vessel competing in or practicing for a regatta or boat race over a specified course held by a bona fide club or racing association, provided that due written notice of the date of the race has been given to the appropriate law enforcement agency at least fifteen days prior to such race, pursuant to the provisions of section thirty-four of this chapter, and all provisions of this section have been complied with.

3. Any person who operates a vessel in violation of any of the provisions of this section shall be guilty of a violation punishable as set forth in section seventy-three-c of this article.

4. Nothing in this section shall be construed as prohibiting any town or county from continuing, adopting or enacting any other local laws, resolutions or ordinances related to persons operating a vessel within its limits, but no such municipality shall have the power to make less restrictive any of such provisions.

§ 46. Vessel regulation zone

1.

(a) The board of supervisors or other legislative governing body of a county, or, should no action on the matter be taken by such board or body, the governing body of a city or incorporated village, by a three-quarters vote of its members, may establish a vessel regulation zone and within the limitations prescribed by this chapter, adopt regulations for the use of a lake or part of a lake or other body of water within the county, or in case of a city or incorporated village of the part of said waters adjacent thereto, if it shall deem that such establishment of a zone will promote the safety of the people and be for the best interests of the county, city or incorporated village.

(b) The governing body of a city or incorporated village, by a three-quarters vote of its members, may establish a personal watercraft and specialty prop-craft regulation zone and within the limitations prescribed by this chapter, adopt regulations for the use of a lake or part of a lake or other body of water adjacent to such city or incorporated village, if it shall deem that such establishment of a zone will promote the safety of the people and be for the best interests of the city or incorporated village. With respect to personal watercraft and specialty prop-craft, such regulations may include a prohibition of their use provided such prohibition does not prevent access to federally maintained and designated navigation channels.

2. Before any such zone shall be established, a public hearing shall be held before the members of the board of supervisors or other legislative governing body of the county or the governing body of the city or incorporated village, or a committee designated for that purpose, upon not less than thirty days notice of such hearing published in at least two newspapers having general circulation in the territory affected. Such notice will specify the time and place of hearing, the limits of the proposed zone which shall not exceed fifteen hundred feet from the shore line at low water mark of the body of water where the zone is to be established and the regulations proposed to be adopted. Following such hearing the committee shall report to the board of supervisors, or other legislative governing body of the county or the governing body of the city or incorporated village, and such board or governing body may adopt the limits of the proposed zone and its regulations. It shall be the duty of the clerk of the board of supervisors, or other legislative governing body of the county or the clerk of the governing body of the city or incorporated village to promptly file a certified copy of such established vessel regulation zone and regulations adopted in the office of the clerk of the county wherein such zone is established.

3. When such regulation zones are established there shall be constructed by the county, city or incorporated village establishing same, on the shore near each boundary, a signboard facing the water and bearing thereon in large letters "VESSEL REGULATION ZONE" with the rate of speed limited in that area and/or such other restrictions as may be adopted. Such signboard shall be conspicuously placed. Any expense incurred in the formation or operation of the zone or district shall be a county, city or incorporated village charge and shall be paid for in the same manner as other charges against such political units.

4. Any person violating any of the regulations adopted pursuant to the provisions of this section shall be guilty of a misdemeanor punishable as set forth in section seventy-three-b of this article. The provisions of this section shall not apply to any vessel while actually competing in a duly authorized regatta as provided in section thirty-four of this chapter, and provided due written notice of the date of such race or regatta has been filed with the clerk of the county wherein such vessel regulation zone has been established.

5. It shall be the duty of all peace officers, acting pursuant to their special duties, police officers and traveling navigation inspectors, to enforce the provisions of this section.

§ 46-a. Regulations of vessels

(1) The local legislative body of a city or the board of trustees of a village may adopt, amend and enforce local laws, rules and regulations not inconsistent with the laws of this state or the United States, with respect to:

a. Regulating the speed and regulating and restricting the operation of vessels while being operated or driven upon any waters within or bounding the appropriate city or village, including any waters within or bordering a village in the county of Nassau or Suffolk, to a distance of fifteen hundred feet from the shore.

b. Restricting and regulating the anchoring or mooring of vessels in any waters within or bounding the appropriate city or village to a distance of fifteen hundred feet from the shore.

c. Restricting and regulating the anchoring or mooring of vessels in such waters when used or occupied as living or sleeping quarters and; providing time limits on duration of the stay of such vessels in such waters and requiring inspection and registration of such vessels when so used.

d. Restricting and regulating garbage removal from said vessels.

e. Designating public anchorage area or areas and regulating the use thereof.

(2) The local legislative body of the village of Sodus Point and the town of Huron in the county of Wayne, the villages of Croton-on-Hudson and Mamaroneck and the town of Cortlandt in the county of Westchester, the town of Stony Point in the county of Rockland, the town of Grand Island in the county of Erie, the towns of Conesus, Geneseo, Groveland and Livonia in the county of Livingston, the towns of Irondequoit, Webster, and Penfield in the county of Monroe, the village of Greenwood Lake and the town of Warwick in the county of Orange, the town of Carlton in the county of Orleans, the village of Sackets Harbor in the county of Jefferson, and the villages of Union Springs, Aurora and Cayuga and the towns of Genoa and Ledyard in the county of Cayuga, the town of Ithaca in the county of Tompkins, the city of Kingston and the village of Saugerties in the county of Ulster and the town of Porter in the county of Niagara, the village of North Haven in the county of Suffolk, and the towns of Fayette and Varick in the county of Seneca may adopt, amend and enforce local laws, rules and regulations not inconsistent with the laws of this state or the United States, with respect to the restriction and regulation of the manner of construction and location of boathouses, moorings and docks in any waters within or bounding the respective municipality to a distance of fifteen hundred feet from the shoreline.

(3) [Repealed]

(4)

a. The local legislative body of the city of Canandaigua and the towns of Canandaigua, Gorham, South Bristol, Canadice and Richmond in the county of Ontario and the towns of Middlesex and Italy in the county of Yates may adopt, amend and enforce local laws, rules and regulations not inconsistent with the laws of the United States, with respect to the restriction and regulation of the manner of construction and location of boathouses, moorings and docks in any waters within or bounding the aforementioned cities and towns to a distance of 1500 feet from the shoreline.

b. No such local law, rule or regulation shall take effect in the town of Canandaigua, Gorham, South Bristol, Middlesex or Italy or in the city of Canandaigua with regard to Canandaigua Lake, or in the town of Canadice or Richmond with regard to Honeoye Lake until all respective lakeshore municipalities unanimously agree by resolution to a set of uniform standards that include at a minimum the length and density of docks, the number of boats or boat slips allowed per lineal foot of lakeshore for various land uses, the number of moorings and boathouses allowed for various land uses, and the allowable dimensions and locations for docks, and provided further that no such local law shall take effect until it shall have been submitted to and approved in writing by the commissioner of parks, recreation and historic preservation and provided further that no future amendments to the uniform standards shall take effect until all respective lakeshore municipalities unanimously agree by resolution to the revised set of uniform standards and such revised standards have similarly been submitted to and approved in writing by the commissioner.

(5) The local legislative body of any city, town or village which is a participating community as defined in subdivision ten of section 44-0103 of the environmental conservation law may adopt, amend and enforce local laws, rules and regulations not inconsistent with the laws of this state or the United States or with the Hudson river valley greenway compact, with respect to the restriction and regulation of the manner of construction and location of boathouses, moorings and docks in any waters within or bounding the respective municipality to a distance of fifteen hundred feet from the shoreline. Nothing in this subdivision or in article forty-four of the environmental conservation law or in the Hudson river valley greenway compact produced pursuant to such article, shall be deemed to affect, impair or supersede the provisions of any charter, local law, rule or other local requirements and procedures heretofore or hereafter adopted by such participating community, including, but not limited to, any such provisions relating to the zoning and use of land or any waters within or bounding such participating community to a distance of fifteen hundred feet from the shoreline.

(6)

a. The local legislative bodies of the towns of Barrington, Jerusalem, Milo, Pulteney, Urbana and Wayne and the villages of Hammondsport and Penn Yan in the counties of Steuben and Yates may adopt, amend and enforce local laws, rules and regulations not inconsistent with the laws of the United States, with respect to the restriction and regulation of the manner of construction and location of boathouses, moorings and docks in any waters within or bounding the aforementioned towns and villages to a distance of fifteen hundred feet from the shoreline.

b. No such local law, rule or regulation shall take effect in the towns of Barrington, Jerusalem, Milo, Pulteney, Urbana or Wayne and the villages of Hammondsport and Penn Yan with regard to Keuka Lake, until all respective lakeshore municipalities unanimously agree by resolution to a set of uniform standards that include at a minimum the length and density of docks, the number of boats or boat slips allowed per lineal foot of lakeshore for various land uses, the number of moorings and boathouses allowed for various land uses, and the allowable dimensions and locations for docks, and provided further that no such local law shall take effect until it shall have been submitted to and approved in writing by the commissioner and provided further that no future amendments to the uniform standards shall take effect until all respective lakeshore municipalities unanimously agree by resolution to the revised set of uniform standards and such revised standards have similarly been submitted to and approved in writing by the commissioner.

The provisions of this section shall be controlling notwithstanding any contrary provisions of law.

§ 46-aa. Special provisions relating to speed on lakes in Chautauqua county

1. The county legislature of the county of Chautauqua may adopt, amend and enforce local laws, rules and regulations not inconsistent with the laws of this state or the United States, with respect to regulating and restricting the rate of speed of vessels while being operated on any navigable waters, or part thereof, located within Chautauqua county, including, but not limited to regulating or restricting the operation of vessels within two hundred feet of the shore, a dock, pier, raft or float or an anchored or moored vessel in a manner or at a speed that does not cause a wake that unreasonably interferes with or endangers such dock, pier, raft or float or an anchored or moored vessel but in no event at a speed exceeding five miles per hour, unless for the purpose of enabling a person engaged in water skiing to take off or land, or regulating or restricting the speed of vessels on such lake between one-half hour after sunset and one-half hour before sunrise.

2. Local laws, rules and regulations adopted pursuant to the provisions of this section shall not apply to any pleasure vessel competing in or practicing for a regatta or boat race over a specified course held by a bona fide club or racing association, provided that due written

notice of the date of the race has been given to the appropriate law enforcement agency at least fifteen days prior to such race, pursuant to the provisions of section thirty-four of this chapter, and all provisions of such section have been complied with.

3. No local law, rule or regulation adopted pursuant to the provisions of this section shall take effect until it shall have been submitted to and approved in writing by the commissioner of parks, recreation and historic preservation.

Nothing in this section shall be construed as prohibiting any city, town or village from continuing, adopting or enacting any other local laws relating to persons operating a vessel within its limits, but no such municipality shall have the power to make less restrictive any of such provisions than any local law, rule or regulation which may be adopted pursuant to provisions of this section.

§ 46-aaa. Special provisions relating to reckless operation and speed on certain lakes in Hamilton county

1. Notwithstanding any other provisions of this chapter or any inconsistent local laws (a) every pleasure vessel operated on Blue Mountain lake, Eagle lake, Indian lake, and Utowana lake, shall be operated in a careful and prudent manner, in such a way as not to unreasonably interfere with or endanger any vessel or person; a violation of this paragraph shall be a misdemeanor punishable as set forth in section seventy-three-b of this article; and (b) no vessel shall be operated on such lakes at a speed exceeding forty-five miles per hour nor shall any pleasure vessel be operated at a speed exceeding twenty-five miles per hour between one-half hour after sunset and one-half hour before sunrise; a violation of this paragraph shall be a violation punishable as set forth in section seventy-three-c of this article.

2. No vessel shall be operated on Blue Mountain lake, Eagle lake, Indian lake and Utowana lake within two hundred feet of the shore, a dock, pier, raft or float or an anchored or moored vessel in a manner or at such a speed that causes a wake that unreasonably interferes with or endangers such dock, pier, raft or float or an anchored or moored vessel but in no event at a speed exceeding five miles per hour, unless for the purpose of enabling a person engaged in water skiing to take off or land. A violation of this subdivision is a violation punishable as set forth in section seventy-three-c of this article.

3. The provisions of this section shall not apply to any vessel competing in or practicing for a regatta or boat race over a specified course held by a bona fide club or racing association, provided that due written notice of the date of the race has been given to the appropriate law enforcement agencies at least fifteen days prior to such race, pursuant to the provisions of section thirty-four of this chapter, and all provisions of such section have been complied with. The provisions of this section shall not apply to any Federal Aviation Agency licensed aircraft.

4. Nothing in this section shall be construed as prohibiting any town or county from adopting or enacting any local laws, resolutions or ordinances related to persons operating a vessel within its limits, but no such municipality shall have the power to make less restrictive any of such provisions.

§ 46-aaaa. Special provisions relating to speed on Cuba lake

1. Notwithstanding any other provisions of this chapter or any inconsistent local laws, every pleasure vessel operated on Cuba lake, located in the towns of Cuba, Allegany county and Ischua, Cattaraugus county, shall be operated in a careful and prudent manner, in such a way as to not unreasonably interfere with or endanger any vessel or person, and no vessel shall be operated at a speed exceeding forty-five miles per hour. No pleasure vessel operated on Cuba lake shall be operated at a speed exceeding twenty-five miles per hour between one-half hour after sunset and one-half hour before sunrise.

2. No person shall ride on water skis, surfboard, motorized jet ski or motorized personal watercraft or similar device on the waters of Cuba lake, without wearing a life preserver, life belt, or similar device; provided, however, that the provisions of this subdivision shall not apply to a paid performer engaged in a professional exhibition.

3. The provisions of this section shall not apply to any vessel competing in or practicing for a regatta or boat race over a specified course held by a bona fide club or racing association, provided that due written notice of the date of the race has been given to the appropriate law enforcement agencies at least fifteen days prior to such race, pursuant to the provisions of section thirty-four of this chapter, and all provisions of this section have been complied with. The provisions of this section shall not apply to any Federal Aviation Agency licensed aircraft.

4. Any person who fails to comply with any of the provisions of this section shall be guilty of a violation punishable by a fine of not less than twenty-five dollars nor more than one hundred dollars for the first offense; by a fine of not less than fifty dollars nor more than two hundred dollars for conviction of the second offense committed within a period of twenty-four months; by a fine of not less than one hundred dollars nor more than two hundred dollars for conviction of the third offense or any subsequent offense committed within a period of twenty-four months.

5. The Cuba lake district shall have all of the rights, duties and obligations as provided for in section forty-six of this chapter as afforded to the governing body of a city or incorporated village relative to the creation of a vessel regulation zone.

§ 46-b. Special provisions relating to speed on Saratoga lake

1. Notwithstanding any other provisions of this chapter or any inconsistent local laws, every pleasure vessel operated on Saratoga lake, located in the towns of Malta, Saratoga and Stillwater, and the city of Saratoga Springs, Saratoga county, shall be operated in a careful and prudent manner, in such a way as to not unreasonably interfere with or endanger any vessel or person, and no vessel shall be operated at a speed exceeding forty-five miles per hour. No pleasure vessel operated on Saratoga lake shall be operated at a speed exceeding twenty-five miles per hour between one-half hour after sunset and one-half hour before sunrise.

2. In addition to the waters of Saratoga lake, the provisions of this section shall apply to Fish creek from Saratoga lake to Safford's bridge. Notwithstanding subdivision one of this section the five miles per hour speed zone at the state route nine-P state boat launch, in effect prior to the effective date of this section, shall remain in full force and effect.

3. No vessel shall be operated on Saratoga lake within two hundred feet of shore, a dock, pier, raft or float or an anchored or moored vessel in a manner or at such a speed that causes a wake that unreasonably interferes with or endangers such shoreline, dock, pier, raft or float or anchored or moored vessel, but in no event at a speed exceeding five miles per hour, unless for the purpose of enabling a person engaged in water skiing to take off or land.

4. The provisions of this section shall not apply to any vessel competing in or practicing

for a regatta or boat race over a specified course held by a bona fide club or racing association, provided that due written notice of the date of the race has been given to the appropriate law enforcement agencies at least fifteen days prior to such race, pursuant to the provisions of section thirty-four of this chapter, and all provisions of such section have been complied with. The provisions of this section shall not apply to any federal aviation agency licensed aircraft.

5. Any person who violates any provision of this section shall be guilty of a violation punishable as provided in section seventy-three-c of this article.

§ 47. Leaving the scene of an accident without reporting

1.

(a) Whenever any vessel, including, but not limited to, rowboats, canoes and kayaks, meets with an accident involving damage to any vessel or to the real property or to the personal property, not including animals, of another due to an accident involving such vessel and the operator thereof has knowledge of such accident, such operator shall, before leaving the place where the damage occurred, stop and give his or her name and address, the name and address of the owner thereof and the identification number, if any, assigned to such vessel to the person sustaining the damage. In the event the person sustaining the damage cannot be located at the place where the damage occurred, then the operator of such vessel shall report the same as soon as physically able to the nearest police officer, police station, bay constable or judicial officer.

(b) A violation of the provisions of paragraph (a) of this subdivision shall constitute a violation punishable as set forth in section seventy-three-c of this article.

2.

(a) Every operator of a vessel, including, but not limited to, rowboats, canoes and kayaks, who, knowing or having cause to know that personal injury has been caused to another person, or another person has disappeared under the water, due to an accident involving such vessel shall, before leaving the place where the said incident involving personal injury occurred, stop, give such operator's name and address, the name and address of the owner of such vessel and the identification number, if any, assigned to such vessel to the injured party, if practical, and shall report said accident as soon as physically able to the nearest police officer, police station, bay constable or judicial officer.

(b) The first violation of the provisions of paragraph (a) of this subdivision involving personal injury to another person resulting solely from the failure of a vessel operator to provide the name and address of the vessel owner and/or the identification number of the vessel shall constitute a class B misdemeanor punishable by a fine of not less than two hundred fifty nor more than five hundred dollars in addition to any other penalties provided by law. Any subsequent such violation after a conviction for such violation within the preceding five years shall constitute a class A misdemeanor punishable by a fine of not less than five hundred nor more than one thousand dollars in addition to any other penalties provided by law. Any violation of the provisions of paragraph (a) of this subdivision, other than the mere failure of a vessel operator to provide the name and address of the vessel owner and/or the identification number of the vessel, shall constitute a class A misdemeanor, punishable by a fine of not less than five hundred nor more than one thousand dollars in addition to any other penalties provided by law. Any such violation committed by a person after such person has previously been convicted of such a violation shall constitute a class E felony, punishable by a fine of not less than one thousand nor more than two thousand five hundred dollars in addition to any other penalties provided by law. Any violation of the provisions of paragraph (a) of this subdivision, other than the mere failure of a vessel operator to provide the name and address of the vessel owner and/or the identification number of the vessel where the personal injury involved (i) results in serious physical injury, as defined in section 10.00 of the penal law, or where a person has disappeared under the water as the result of the incident shall constitute a class E felony or (ii) results in death shall constitute a class D felony.

3. The provisions of this section shall not apply to commercial vessels having a valid marine document issued by the United States or a foreign government.

§ 47-a. Accidents; police authorities, bay constables and coroners to report

1. Every police officer, bay constable or judicial officer receiving information of an accident involving a vessel, including, but not limited to, rowboats and canoes, in which any person is killed, injured or disappears under the water shall immediately investigate the facts, or cause the same to be investigated, make a written memorandum of the information received,

and such additional facts relating to the accident as may come to his or her knowledge, and mail the same within five days to the commissioner and keep a record thereof in his or her office, provided, however, that the report of the accident is made to the police officer, bay constable or judicial officer within five days after such accident. Every coroner, or other official performing like functions, shall likewise make a report to the commissioner with respect to all deaths found to have been the result of vessel accidents.

2. Every police officer, bay constable or judicial officer receiving information of an accident involving a vessel, including, but not limited to, rowboats and canoes, in which damage in excess of one thousand dollars to the property of any person is sustained shall make a written memorandum of the information received, and such additional facts relating to the accident as may come to his or her knowledge, and mail the same within five days to the commissioner and keep a record thereof in his or her office.

3. In accordance with any request duly made by an authorized official or agency of the United States, any information compiled by or otherwise available to the commissioner pursuant to this section shall be transmitted to such official or agency of the United States.

§ 47-b. Report to the commissioner required upon accident

Every person operating a vessel, including, but not limited to, rowboats and canoes, upon the navigable waters of the state, or on any other waters within the boundaries of the state, which is in any manner involved in an accident, in which any person is killed, injured or disappears under the water, or in which damage to the property of any one person, including himself or herself, in excess of one thousand dollars is sustained shall, within five days after such accident, report the matter in writing to the commissioner. If the owner is not involved in such accident or is incapacitated, the owner shall, within five days after learning of the facts of such accident, report the matter to the commissioner together with such information as may have come to the owner's knowledge relating to such accident. Every such operator of a vessel, or surviving participant in any such accident, or the owner of the vessel involved in any such accident, shall make such other and additional reports as the commissioner may require. A violation of this section shall constitute a violation punishable by a fine of not less than twenty-five nor more than one hundred dollars. Nothing contained in this section shall be deemed to supersede the provisions of section forty-seven of this article.

§ 48. Negligence in use or operation of vessel attributable to owner

1. Every owner of a vessel used or operated upon the navigable waters of the state or any tidewaters bordering on or lying within the boundaries of Nassau and Suffolk counties, shall be liable and responsible for death or injuries to person or property resulting from negligence in the use or operation of such vessel, in the business of such owner, or otherwise, by any person using or operating the same with the permission, express or implied, of such owner.

The use or operation by a non-resident or non-residents of a vessel in this state, or the use or operation in this state of a vessel in the business of a non-resident, or the use or operation in this state of a vessel owned by a non-resident if so used or operated with his permission, express or implied, shall be deemed equivalent to an appointment by such non-resident of the secretary of state to be his true and lawful attorney upon whom may be served the summons in any action against him, growing out of any accident or collision in which such non-resident may be involved while using or operating such vessel in this state or in which such vessel may be involved while being used or operated in this state in the business of such non-resident or with the permission, express or implied, of such non-resident owner; and such use or operation shall be a signification of his agreement that any such summons against him which is so served shall be of the same legal force and validity as if served on him personally within the state and within the territorial jurisdiction of the court from which the summons issues, and that such appointment of the secretary of state shall be irrevocable and binding upon his executor or administrator. Where such non-resident has died prior to the commencement of an action brought pursuant to this section, service of process shall be made on the executor or administrator of such non-resident in the same manner and on the same notice as is provided in the case of the non-resident himself. Where an action has been duly commenced under the provisions of this section against a non-resident who dies thereafter, the court must allow the action to be continued against his executor or administrator upon motion with such notice as the court may deem proper.

2. A summons in an action described in this section may issue in any court in the state having jurisdiction of the subject matter and be served as hereinafter provided. Service of such summons shall be made by mailing a copy thereof to the secretary of state at his office

in the city of Albany, or by personally delivering a copy thereof to one of his regularly established offices, with a fee of ten dollars, and such service shall be sufficient service upon such non-resident provided that notice of such service and a copy of the summons and complaint are forthwith sent by or on behalf of the plaintiff to the defendant by registered mail with return receipt requested. The plaintiff shall file with the clerk of the court in which the action is pending, or with the judge or justice of such court in case there be no clerk, an affidavit of compliance herewith, a copy of the summons and complaint, and either a return receipt purporting to be signed by the defendant or a person qualified to receive his registered mail, in accordance with the rules an [and]* customs of the post-office department; or, if acceptance was refused by the defendant or his agent, the original envelope bearing a notation by the postal authorities that receipt was refused, and an affidavit by or on behalf of the plaintiff that notice of such mailing and refusal was forthwith sent to the defendant by ordinary mail. Where the summons is mailed to a foreign country, other official proof of the delivery of the mail may be filed in case the post-office department is unable to obtain such a return receipt. The foregoing papers shall be filed within thirty days after the return receipt or other official proof of delivery or the original envelope bearing a notation of refusal, as the case may be, is received by the plaintiff. Service of process shall be complete ten days after such papers are filed. The return receipt or other official proof of delivery shall constitute presumptive evidence that the summons mailed was received by the defendant or a person qualified to receive his registered mail; and the notation or refusal shall constitute presumptive evidence that the refusal was by the defendant or his agent. Service of such summons also may be made by mailing a copy thereof to the secretary of state at this [his]* office in the city of Albany, or by personally delivering a copy thereof to one of his regularly established offices, with a fee of ten dollars, and by delivering a duplicate copy thereof, with the complaint annexed thereto, to the defendant personally without the state by a resident or citizen of the state of New York or a sheriff, under-sheriff, deputy-sheriff or constable of the county or other political subdivision in which the personal service is made, or an officer authorized by the laws of this state, to take acknowledgements of deeds to be recorded in this state, or an attorney and/or counselor at law, solicitor, advocate or barrister duly qualified to practice in the state or country where such service is made, or by a United States marshal or deputy United States marshal. Proof of personal service without the state shall be filed with the clerk of the court in which the action is pending within thirty days after such service. Personal service without the state is complete ten days after proof thereof is filed. The court in which the action is pending may order such extensions as may be necessary to afford the defendant reasonable opportunity to defend the action.

Nothing herein shall be construed as affecting other methods of service of process against non-residents as provided by law.

3. As used in this section "vessel" means a vessel as defined in section two, subdivision six of this chapter, except a vessel having a valid marine document issued by the United States or a foreign government.

4. As used in this section, "owner" means any person other than a lien holder having the property in or title to a vessel, and also any lessee or bailee having the exclusive use thereof, under a lease or otherwise, for a period greater than thirty days, and their liability under this section, shall be joint and several. If a vessel be sold under a contract of conditional sale whereby the title to such vessel remains in the vendor, such vendor or his assignee shall not, after delivery of such vessel, be deemed an owner within the provisions of this section, but the vendee or his assignee, receiving possession thereof, shall be deemed such owner notwithstanding the terms of such contract, until the vendor or his assignee shall retake possession of such vessel. A chattel mortgagee, conditional vendor, or an entruster as defined by section fifty-one*of the personal property law, of any vessel out of possession, shall not be deemed an owner within the provisions of this section.

5. All bonds executed by or policies of insurance issued to the owner of any vessel subject to the provisions of this section shall contain a provision for indemnity or security against the liability and responsibility provided in this section; but this provision shall not be construed as requiring that such a policy include insurance against any liability of the insured, being an individual, for death of or injuries to his or her spouse or injury to property of either.

6. This section shall not be construed to affect any of the rights of an owner under the laws of the United States.

§ 49. Operator

1. No person born on or after May first, nineteen hundred ninety-six shall operate a mechanically propelled vessel on the navigable waters of the state or any tidewaters bordering on or lying within the boundaries of Nassau and Suffolk counties, unless:

a. the operator is at least ten years old and is the holder of a boating safety certificate issued to him or her by the commissioner, the United States Power Squadrons, the United States coast guard auxiliary or the United States sailing association for a powerboating course or courses which are approved by the commissioner; or

b. the operator is younger than eighteen years of age, and is accompanied on the mechanically propelled vessel by at least one person who is at least eighteen years of age and is

(i) the holder of a boating safety certificate issued to him or her by the commissioner, the United States Power Squadrons, the United States coast guard auxiliary or the United States sailing association for a powerboating course or courses which are approved by the commissioner, or

(ii) not required by this subdivision to hold a boating safety certificate in order to operate a mechanically propelled vessel; or

c. the operator is eighteen years of age or older, is a person required by this subdivision to hold a boating safety certificate in order to operate a mechanically propelled vessel, and is accompanied on the mechanically propelled vessel by at least one person who is at least eighteen years of age and the holder of a boating safety certificate; or

d. the operator is the owner of a recently purchased vessel and may operate such vessel without the otherwise required boating safety certificate for a period of time not to exceed one hundred twenty days from the date of purchase.

e. The provisions of this subdivision shall not apply to persons who are: born before April thirtieth, nineteen hundred ninety-six; certified by the commissioner as boating safety instructors; members of the United States Power Squadrons; members of the United States coast guard auxiliary; holders of public vessel licenses pursuant to section sixty-four of this article; police officers, peace officers, fire personnel, rescue personnel or lifeguards, when any such person is acting pursuant to assigned duties; or licensed to operate vessels by the

United States coast guard or the Canadian coast guard. The commissioner, by rule or regulation, may provide for the exemption of additional persons not listed in this paragraph from the requirements of this section.

f. The provisions of this subdivision shall supersede all local laws or ordinances relating to requirements for boating safety certificates to operate a mechanically propelled vessel.

1-a.

a. No person shall operate a personal watercraft or specialty prop-craft upon the navigable waters of the state or any tidewaters bordering on or lying within the boundaries of Nassau and Suffolk counties unless the operator is fourteen years of age or older and the holder of, or is accompanied by a person over eighteen years of age who is the holder of a boating safety certificate issued by the commissioner, the United States power squadrons, the United States coast guard auxiliary, the United States sailing association for a powerboating course or courses which are approved by the commissioner, or other state or government, as a result of completing a course approved by the commissioner.

b. No person who is the owner of a personal watercraft or specialty prop-craft shall knowingly authorize or permit the operation thereof on the navigable waters of the state or any tidewaters bordering on or lying within the boundaries of Nassau or Suffolk counties unless the operator is fourteen years of age or older and the holder of, or is accompanied by a person over eighteen years of age who is the holder of a boating safety certificate issued by the commissioner, the United States power squadrons, United States coast guard auxiliary, the United States sailing association for a powerboating course or courses which are approved by the commissioner, or other state or government, as a result of completing a course approved by the commissioner.

c. For the purposes of this subdivision "accompanied" shall mean upon the vessel.

d. The provisions of this subdivision shall not apply to persons: certified by the commissioner as boating safety instructors; members of the United States power squadrons; members of the United States coast guard auxiliary; holders of public vessel licenses pursuant to section sixty-four of this article; police officers acting pursuant to assigned duties; peace officers acting pursuant to assigned duties; lifeguards acting pursuant to assigned duties; fire and rescue personnel acting pursuant to assigned duties; and persons licensed to operate vessels by the United States coast guard or the Canadian coast guard. The commissioner by rule and regulation may provide for the exemption of additional persons not listed in this paragraph from the requirements of this section.

2. The failure of a person specified in subdivision one or one-a of this section, to exhibit a boating safety certificate upon demand to any magistrate, peace officer, acting pursuant to his or her special duties, police officer, inspector of the state office of parks, recreation and historic preservation, traveling navigation inspector or other officer having authority to enforce the provisions of this chapter, shall be presumptive evidence that such person is not the holder of such certificate.

3. No person who is the owner of a mechanically propelled vessel shall knowingly authorize or permit the operation thereof on the navigable waters of the state or any tidewaters bordering on or lying within the boundaries of Nassau and Suffolk counties, unless:

a. the operator is born on or before April thirtieth, nineteen hundred ninety-six; or,

b. the operator is born on or after May first, nineteen hundred ninety-six, is at least ten years of age and is the holder of a boating safety certificate issued to him or her by the commissioner, the United States Power Squadrons, the United States coast guard auxiliary, or the United States sailing association for a powerboating course or courses which are approved by the commissioner, or

c. the operator is younger than eighteen years of age, and is accompanied on the mechanically propelled vessel by at least one person eighteen years of age or older and is:

(i) the holder of a boating safety certificate issued to him or her by the commissioner, the United States Power Squadrons, the United States coast guard auxiliary, or the United States sailing association for a powerboating course or courses which are approved by the commissioner, or

(ii) not required by subdivision one of this section to hold a boating safety certificate in order to operate a mechanically propelled vessel; or

d. the operator is eighteen years of age or older, is a person required by subdivision one of this section to hold a boating safety certificate in order to operate a mechanically propelled vessel, and is accompanied by a person who is at least eighteen years of age and is the holder of a boating safety certificate.

e. The provisions of this subdivision shall supersede all local laws or ordinances relating to requirements for boating safety certificates to operate a mechanically propelled vessel.

4. Whenever any police officer or peace officer authorized to enforce the provisions of this chapter having reasonable cause to believe that a person is operating a vessel in violation of section forty-nine-a of this article, or any other provision of this article for which a suspension may be imposed, such officer may demand of such person his or her name, address and an explanation of his or her conduct.

5. The provisions of subdivisions one, one-a and two of this section shall not apply while the operator is actually preparing for or competing in a regatta or boat race authorized under section thirty-four of this chapter or for which a marine event permit has been issued by the United States coast guard.

6. No person operating a vessel upon the navigable waters of the state or on the tidewaters bordering on and lying within the boundaries of Nassau or Suffolk county shall fail or refuse to comply with any lawful order or direction of any police officer or peace officer acting pursuant to his or her special duties. Failure or refusal to comply with such lawful order or direction shall be a violation punishable as provided for in subdivision seven of this section.

7. A violation of subdivision one, one-a, two or six of this section shall constitute a violation punishable as set forth in section seventy-three-c of this article.

§ 49-a. Operation of a vessel while under the influence of alcohol or drugs

1. Definitions. As used in this section, unless the context clearly indicates otherwise:

(a) The term "vessel" shall be every description of watercraft or other artificial contrivance propelled in whole or in part by mechanical power and, which is used or capable of being used as a means of transportation over water, and which is underway and not at anchor or made fast to the shore or ground. The term "vessel" shall include a "public vessel" as defined herein unless otherwise specified.

(b) The term "public vessel" shall mean and include every vessel which is propelled in whole or in part by mechanical power and is used or operated for commercial purposes on the navigable waters of the state; that is either carrying passengers, carrying freight, towing, or for any other use, for which a compensation is received, either directly or where provided as an accommodation, advantage, facility or privilege at any place of public accommodation, resort or amusement.

(c) The term "waters of the state" means all of the waterways or bodies of water located within New York state or that part of any body of water which is adjacent to New York state over which the state has territorial jurisdiction, on which a vessel or public vessel may be used or operated, including Nassau and Suffolk counties.

2. Offenses: criminal penalties.

(a) No person shall operate a vessel upon the waters of the state while his or her ability to operate such vessel is impaired by the consumption of alcohol. (1) A violation of this subdivision shall be an offense and shall be punishable by a fine of not less than three hundred dollars nor more than five hundred dollars, or by imprisonment in a penitentiary or county jail for not more than fifteen days, or by both such fine and imprisonment. (2) A person who operates a vessel in violation of this subdivision after being convicted of a violation of any subdivision of this section within the preceding five years shall be punished by a fine of not less than five hundred dollars nor more than seven hundred fifty dollars, or by imprisonment of not more than thirty days in a penitentiary or county jail or by both such fine and imprisonment. (3) A person who operates a vessel in violation of this subdivision after being convicted two or more times of a violation of any subdivision of this section within the preceding ten years shall be guilty of a misdemeanor, and shall be punished by a fine of not less than seven hundred fifty dollars nor more than fifteen hundred dollars, or by imprisonment of not more than one hundred eighty days in a penitentiary or county jail or by both such fine and imprisonment.

(b) No such person shall operate a vessel other than a public vessel while he has .08 of one per centum or more by weight of alcohol in his blood, breath, urine, or saliva, as determined by the chemical test made pursuant to the provisions of subdivision seven of this section.

(c) No such person shall operate a public vessel while he has .04 of one per centum or more by weight of alcohol in his blood, breath, urine, or saliva, as determined by the chemical test made pursuant to the provisions of subdivision seven of this section.

(d) No person shall operate a vessel while he is in an intoxicated condition.

(e) No person shall operate a vessel while his ability to operate such vessel is impaired by the use of a drug as defined by section one hundred fourteen-a of the vehicle and traffic law.

(f) (1) A violation of paragraph (b), (c), (d) or (e) of this subdivision shall be a misdemeanor and shall be punishable by imprisonment in a penitentiary or county jail for not more than one year, or by a fine of not less than five hundred dollars nor more than one thousand dollars, or by both such fine and imprisonment. (2) A person who operates a vessel in violation of paragraph (b), (c), (d) or (e) of this subdivision after having been convicted of a violation of paragraph (b), (c), (d) or (e) of this subdivision, or of operating a vessel or public vessel while intoxicated or while under the influence of drugs, within the preceding ten years, shall be guilty of a class E felony and shall be punished by a period of imprisonment as provided in the penal law, or by a fine of not less than one thousand dollars nor more than five thousand dollars, or by both such fine and imprisonment. (3) A person who operates a vessel in violation of paragraph (b), (c), (d) or (e) of this subdivision after having been twice convicted of a violation of any of such paragraph (b), (c), (d) or (e) of this subdivision or of operating a vessel or public vessel while intoxicated or under the influence of drugs, within the preceding ten years, shall be guilty of a class D felony and shall be punished by a fine of not less than two thousand dollars nor more than ten thousand dollars or by a period of imprisonment as provided in the penal law, or by both such fine and imprisonment.

3. Privilege to operate a vessel; suspensions.

(a) The court shall suspend a person's privilege to operate a vessel and may suspend a vessel registration for:

(1) a period of at least six but less than twelve months where an operator is convicted of a violation of paragraph (a) of subdivision two of this section. In determining the length of such suspension or suspensions, the court may take into consideration the seriousness of the offense and may impose a period of suspension whereby such suspension may be in effect during a portion of the current or subsequent boating season;

(2) a period of twelve months where an operator is convicted of a violation of paragraph (b), (c), (d) or (e) of subdivision two of this section;

(3) a period of twenty-four months where a person is convicted of a violation of paragraph (b), (c), (d) or (e) of subdivision two of this section after having been convicted of a violation of paragraph (b), (c), (d) or (e) of subdivision two of this section or of operating a vessel or

public vessel while intoxicated or under the influence of drugs within the preceding ten years.

(b)   The court shall report each conviction recorded pursuant to this section to the commissioner of motor vehicles and the commissioner of parks, recreation and historic preservation on forms provided by the department of motor vehicles. Such reports shall include the length of any suspension imposed on the privilege to operate a vessel and any suspension imposed against a vessel registration. The department of motor vehicles shall maintain a record of all convictions and suspensions in order to effectuate the provisions of this section.

4.

(a)   Operation of vessel while operating privileges have been suspended. No person shall operate a vessel upon the waters of the state while operating privileges have been suspended pursuant to this section or section forty-nine-b of this article. A violation of the provisions of this paragraph shall be a violation and shall be punishable by a fine of not less than three hundred fifty dollars nor more than seven hundred fifty dollars or by imprisonment for a period of not more than ninety days, or by both such fine and imprisonment.

(b)   A person who is in violation of the provisions of paragraph (a) of this subdivision, and in addition is in violation of the provisions of any paragraph of subdivision two of this section arising out of the same incident, shall be guilty of a misdemeanor punishable by a fine of not less than five hundred dollars nor more than five thousand dollars or by a period of imprisonment for a period of not more than one year or by both such fine and imprisonment.

5.   Sentencing limitations. Notwithstanding any provision of the penal law, no judge or magistrate shall impose a sentence of unconditional discharge for a violation of paragraph (b), (c), (d) or (e) of subdivision two of this section nor shall he or she impose a sentence of conditional discharge unless such conditional discharge is accompanied by a sentence of a fine as provided in this section.

5-a.   Sentencing; previous convictions. When sentencing a person for a violation of paragraph (b), (c), (d) or (e) of subdivision two of this section pursuant to subparagraph two of paragraph (f) of subdivision two of this section, the court shall consider any prior convictions the person may have for a violation of subdivision two, two-a three, four, or four-a of section eleven hundred ninety-two of the vehicle and traffic law within the preceding ten years. When sentencing a person for a violation of paragraph (b), (c), (d) or (e) of subdivision two of this section pursuant to subparagraph three of paragraph (f) of subdivision two of this section, the court shall consider any prior convictions the person may have for a violation of subdivision two, two-a, three, four, or four-a of section eleven hundred ninety-two of the vehicle and traffic law within the preceding ten years. When sentencing a person for a violation of subparagraph two of paragraph (a) of subdivision two of this section, the court shall consider any prior convictions the person may have for a violation of any subdivision of section eleven hundred ninety-two of the vehicle and traffic law within the preceding five years. When sentencing a person for a violation of subparagraph three of paragraph (a) of subdivision two of this section, the court shall consider any prior convictions the person may have for a violation of any subdivision of section eleven hundred ninety-two of the vehicle and traffic law within the preceding ten years.

6. Arrest and testing.

(a) Notwithstanding the provisions of section 140.10 of the criminal procedure law, a police officer may, without a warrant, arrest a person, in case of a violation of any paragraph of subdivision two of this section, if such violation is coupled with an accident or collision in which such person is involved, which in fact had been committed, though not in the police officer's presence, when he has reasonable cause to believe that the violation was committed by such person. For the purposes of this subdivision police officer shall also include a peace officer authorized to enforce this chapter when the alleged violation constitutes a crime.

(b) Breath test for operators of vessel. Every person operating a vessel on the waters of the state which has been involved in an accident or which is operated in violation of any of the provisions of this section which regulate the manner in which a vessel is to be properly operated while underway shall, at the request of a police officer, submit to a breath test to be administered by the police officer. If such test indicates that such operator has consumed alcohol, the police officer may request such operator to submit to a chemical test in the manner set forth in subdivision seven of this section. For the purposes of this section, a vessel is being "operated" only when such vessel is underway and is being propelled in whole or in part by mechanical power.

7. Chemical tests.

(a) Any person who operates a vessel on the waters of the state shall be requested to consent to a chemical test of one or more of the following: breath, blood, urine, or saliva for the purpose of determining the alcoholic or drug content of his blood, provided that such test is administered at the direction of a police officer: (1) having reasonable cause to believe such person to have been operating in violation of this subdivision or paragraph (a), (b), (c), (d) or (e) of subdivision two of this section and within two hours after such person has been placed under arrest for any such violation or (2) within two hours after a breath test as provided in paragraph (b) of subdivision six of this section indicates that alcohol has been consumed by such person and in accordance with the rules and regulations established by the police force of which the officer is a member.

(b) If such person having been placed under arrest or after a breath test indicates the presence of alcohol in the person's system and having thereafter been requested to submit to such chemical test and having been informed that the person's privilege to operate a vessel shall be immediately suspended for refusal to submit to such chemical test or any portion thereof, whether or not the person is found guilty of the charge for which such person is arrested, refuses to submit to such chemical test or any portion thereof, unless a court order has been granted pursuant to subdivision eight of this section, the test shall not be given and a written report of such refusal shall be immediately made by the police officer before whom such refusal was made. Such report may be verified by having the report sworn to, or by affixing to such report a form notice that false statements made therein are punishable as a class A misdemeanor pursuant to section 210.45 of the penal law and such form notice together with the subscription of the deponent shall constitute a verification of the report. The report of the police officer shall set forth reasonable grounds to believe such arrested person to have been operating a vessel in violation of any paragraph of subdivision two of this section, that said person had refused to submit to such chemical test, and that no chemical test was administered pursuant to the requirements of subdivision eight of this section. The report shall be presented to the court upon the arraignment of the arrested person. The privilege to operate a vessel shall, upon the basis of such written report, be temporarily suspended by the court without notice pending the determination of a hearing as provided herein. Copies of such report must be transmitted by the court to the commissioner of parks, recreation and historic preservation and the commissioner of motor vehicles and such transmittal may not be waived even with the consent of all the parties. Such report shall be forwarded to each commissioner within forty-eight hours of such arraignment. The court shall provide such person with a hearing date schedule, a waiver form, and such other information as may be required by the commissioner of motor vehicles. If a hearing, as provided for in paragraph (c) of this subdivision, is waived by such person, the commissioner of motor vehicles shall immediately suspend the privilege to operate a vessel, as of the date of receipt of such waiver in accordance with the provisions of paragraph (d) of this subdivision.

(c) Any person whose privilege to operate a vessel has been suspended pursuant to paragraph (b) of this subdivision is entitled to a hearing in accordance with a hearing schedule to be promulgated by the commissioner of motor vehicles. If the department fails to provide for such hearing fifteen days after the date of the arraignment of the arrested person, the privilege to operate a vessel of such person shall be reinstated pending a hearing pursuant to this section. The hearing shall be limited to the following issues: (1) did the police officer have reasonable cause to believe that such person had been operating a vessel in violation of any paragraph of subdivision two of this section; (2) did the police officer make a lawful arrest of such person; (3) was such person given sufficient warning, in clear or unequivocal language, prior to such refusal that such refusal to submit to such chemical test or any portion thereof, would result in the immediate suspension of such person's privilege to operate a vessel whether or not such person is found guilty of the charge for which the arrest was made; and (4) did such person refuse to submit to such chemical test or any portion thereof. If, after such hearing, the hearing officer, acting on behalf of the commissioner of motor vehicles, finds on any one of said issues in the negative, the hearing officer shall immediately terminate any suspension arising from such refusal. If, after such hearing, the hearing officer, acting on behalf of the commissioner of motor vehicles finds all of the issues in the affirmative, such officer shall immediately suspend the privilege to operate a vessel in accordance with the provisions of paragraph (d) of this subdivision. A person who has had the privilege to operate a vessel suspended pursuant to this subdivision may appeal the findings of the hearing officer in accordance with the provisions of article three-A of the vehicle and traffic law. Any person may waive the right to a hearing under this section. Failure by such person to appear for the scheduled hearing shall constitute a waiver of such hearing, provided, however, that such person may petition the commissioner of motor vehicles for a new hearing which shall be held as soon as practicable.

(d)

(1) Any privilege to operate a vessel which has been suspended pursuant to paragraph (c) of this subdivision shall not be restored for six months after such suspension. However, no such privilege shall be restored for at least one year after such suspension in any case where the person was under the age of twenty-one at the time of the offense, has had a prior suspension resulting from refusal to submit to a chemical test pursuant to this subdivision or subdivision six of section forty-nine-b of this article, or has been convicted of a violation of any paragraph of subdivision two of this section not arising out of the same incident, within the five years immediately preceding the date of such suspension; provided, however, a prior finding that a person under the age of twenty-one has refused to submit to a chemical test pursuant to such subdivision six of section forty-nine-b of this article shall have the same effect as a prior finding of a refusal pursuant to this subdivision solely for the purpose of determining the length of any suspension required to be imposed under any provision of this article, provided that the subsequent offense or refusal is committed or occurred prior to the expiration of the retention period for such prior refusal as set forth in paragraph (k) of subdivision one of section two hundred one of the vehicle and traffic law. Notwithstanding any provision of this paragraph to the contrary, any privilege to operate a vessel which has been suspended pursuant to paragraph (c) of this subdivision, where the person was under the age of twenty-one at the time of the refusal, and such person under the age of twenty-one has a prior finding, conviction or youthful offender adjudication resulting from a violation of this section or section forty-nine-b of this article, not arising from the same incident, shall not be restored for at least one year or until such person reaches the age of twenty-one years, whichever is the greater period of time.

(2) Any person whose privilege to operate a vessel is suspended pursuant to the provisions of this subdivision shall also be liable for a civil penalty in the amount of two hundred dollars except that if such suspension is a second or subsequent suspension pursuant to this subdivision issued within a five year period, or such person has been convicted of a violation of any paragraph of subdivision two of this section within the past five years not arising out of the same incident, the civil penalty shall be in the amount of five hundred dollars. The privilege to operate a vessel shall not be restored to such person unless such penalty has been paid. The first one hundred dollars of each penalty collected by the department of motor vehicles pursuant to the provisions of this subdivision shall be paid to the commissioner of motor vehicles for deposit to the general fund and the remainder of all such penalties shall be paid to the commissioner of parks, recreation and historic preservation for deposit in the "I Love NY Waterways" boating safety fund established pursuant to section ninety-seven-nn of the state finance law.

(e) The commissioner of motor vehicles in consultation with the commissioner of parks, recreation and historic preservation shall promulgate such rules and regulations as may be necessary to effectuate the provisions of this subdivision.

(f) Evidence of a refusal to submit to such chemical test shall be admissible in any trial, proceeding or hearing based upon a violation of the provisions of this section, but only upon a showing that the person was given sufficient warning, in clear and unequivocal language, of the effect of such refusal and that the person persisted in his or her refusal.

(g) Upon the request of the person tested, the results of such test shall be made available to him or her.

8. Compulsory chemical tests.

(a) Notwithstanding the provisions of subdivision seven of this section, no person who operates a vessel in the waters of this state may refuse to submit to a chemical test of one or more of the following: breath, blood, urine or saliva, for the purpose of determining the alcoholic and/or drug content of the blood when a court order for such chemical test has been issued in accordance with the provisions of this subdivision.

(b) Upon refusal by any person to submit to a chemical test or any portion thereof as described in paragraph (a) of this subdivision, the test shall not be given unless a police officer or a district attorney, as defined in subdivision thirty-two of section 1.20 of the criminal procedure law, requests and obtains a court order to compel a person to submit to a chemical test to determine the alcoholic or drug content of the person's blood upon a finding of reasonable cause to believe that:

(1) such person was the operator of a vessel and in the course of such operation a person other than the operator was killed or suffered serious physical injury as defined in section 10.00 of the penal law; and

(2)

(i) either such person operated the vessel in violation of any paragraph of subdivision two of this section, or

(ii) a breath test administered by a police officer in accordance with subdivision six of this section indicates that alcohol has been consumed by such person; and

(3) such person has been placed under lawful arrest; and

(4) such person has refused to submit to a chemical test or any portion thereof, requested in accordance with the provisions of subdivision seven of this section or is unable to give consent to such a test.

(c) For the purpose of this subdivision "reasonable cause" shall be determined by viewing the totality of circumstances surrounding the incident which, when taken together, indicate that the operator was operating a vessel in violation of any paragraph of subdivision two of this section. Such circumstances may include, but are not limited to: evidence that the operator was operating a vessel in violation of any provision of this chapter which regulates the manner in which a vessel is to be properly operated while underway at the time of the incident; any visible indication of alcohol or drug consumption or impairment by the operator; any other evidence surrounding the circumstances of the incident which indicates that the operator has been operating a vessel while impaired by the consumption of alcohol or drugs or was intoxicated at the time of the incident.

(d)

(1) An application for a court order to compel submission to a chemical test or any portion thereof, may be made to any supreme court justice, county court judge or district court judge in the judicial district in which the incident occurred, or if the incident occurred in the

city of New York before any supreme court justice or judge of the criminal court of the city of New York. Such application may be communicated by telephone, radio or other means of electronic communication, or in person.

(2) The applicant must provide identification by name and title and must state the purpose of the communication. Upon being advised that an application for a court order to compel submission to a chemical test is being made, the court shall place under oath the applicant and any other person providing information in support of the application as provided in subparagraph three of this paragraph. After being sworn the applicant must state that the person from whom the chemical test was requested was the operator of a vessel and in the course of such operation a person, other than the operator, has been killed or seriously injured and, based upon the totality of circumstances, there is reasonable cause to believe that such person was operating a vessel in violation of any paragraph of subdivision two of this section and, after being placed under lawful arrest such person refused to submit to a chemical test or any portion thereof, in accordance with the provisions of this section or is unable to give consent to such a test or any portion thereof. The applicant must make specific allegations of fact to support such statement. Any other person properly identified, may present sworn allegations of fact in support of the applicant's statement.

(3) Upon being advised that an oral application for a court order to compel a person to submit to a chemical test is being made, a judge or justice shall place under oath the applicant and any other person providing information in support of the application. Such oath or oaths and all of the remaining communication must be recorded, either by means of a voice recording device or verbatim stenographic or verbatim longhand notes. If a voice recording device is used or a stenographic record made, the judge must have the record transcribed, certify to the accuracy of the transcription and file the original record and transcription with the court within seventy-two hours of the issuance of the court order. If the longhand notes are taken, the judge shall subscribe a copy and file it with the court within twenty-four hours of the issuance of the order.

(4) If the court is satisfied that the requirements for the issuance of a court order pursuant to the provisions of paragraph (b) of this subdivision have been met, it may grant the application and issue an order requiring the accused to submit to a chemical test to

determine the alcoholic and/or drug content of his blood and ordering the withdrawal of a blood sample in accordance with the provisions of subdivision nine of this section. When a judge or justice determines to issue an order to compel submission to a chemical test based on an oral application, the applicant therefor shall prepare the order in accordance with the instructions of the judge or justice. In all cases the order shall include the name of the issuing judge or justice, the name of the applicant, and the date and time it was issued. It must be signed by the judge or justice if issued in person, or by the applicant if issued orally.

(5) Any false statement by an applicant or any other person in support of an application for a court order shall subject such person to the offenses for perjury set forth in article two hundred ten of the penal law.

(e) An order issued pursuant to the provisions of this subdivision shall require that a chemical test to determine the alcoholic and/or drug content of the operator's blood must be administered. The provisions of paragraphs (a), (b) and (c) of subdivision nine of this section shall be applicable to any chemical test administered pursuant to this section.

(f) A defendant who has been compelled to submit to a chemical test pursuant to the provisions of this subdivision may move for the suppression of such evidence in accordance with article seven hundred ten of the criminal procedure law on the grounds that the order was obtained and the test administered in violation of the provisions of this subdivision or any other applicable law.

9. Testing procedures.

(a) At the request of a police officer, the following persons may withdraw blood for the purpose of determining the alcohol or drug content therein: (1) a physician, a registered professional nurse or a registered physician's assistant; or (2) under the supervision and at the direction of a physician: a medical laboratory technician or medical technologist as classified by civil service; a phlebotomist; an advanced emergency medical technician as certified by the department of health, or a medical laboratory technician or medical technologist employed by a clinical laboratory approved under title five of article five of the public health law. This limitation shall not apply to the taking of a urine, saliva or breath specimen.

(b) No person entitled to withdraw blood pursuant to paragraph (a) of this subdivision or hospital employing such person and no other employer of such person shall be sued or held liable for any act done or omitted in the course of withdrawing blood at the request of a police officer or peace officer acting pursuant to his special duties pursuant to this subdivision.

(c) Any person who may have a cause of action arising from the withdrawal of blood as aforesaid, for which no personal liability exists under paragraph (b) of this subdivision, may maintain such action against the state if the person entitled to withdraw blood pursuant to paragraph (a) of this subdivision acted at the request of a police officer or peace officer acting pursuant to his special duties, employed by the state, or against the appropriate political subdivision of the state if the person acted at the request of a police officer or peace officer acting pursuant to his special duties, employed by a political subdivision of the state. No action shall be maintained pursuant to this paragraph unless notice of claim is duly filed or served in compliance with law.

(d) Notwithstanding the foregoing provisions of this subdivision, an action may be maintained by the state or a political subdivision thereof against a person entitled to withdraw blood pursuant to paragraph (a) of this subdivision or hospital employing such person for whose act or omission the state or the political subdivision has been held liable under this subdivision to recover damages, not exceeding the amount awarded to the claimant, that may have been sustained by the state or the political subdivision by reason of gross negligence on the part of such person entitled to withdraw blood.

(e) The testimony of any person, other than a physician, entitled to draw blood pursuant to paragraph (a) of this subdivision in respect to any such withdrawal of blood made by him may be received in evidence with the same weight, force and effect as if such withdrawal of blood were made by a physician.

(f) The provisions of paragraphs (b), (c) and (d) of this subdivision shall also apply with regard to any person employed by a hospital as security personnel for any act done or omitted in the course of withdrawing blood at the request of a police officer pursuant to a court order in accordance with this subdivision.

(g) The person tested shall be permitted to choose a physician to administer a chemical test in addition to the one administered at the direction of the police officer.

10. Chemical test evidence.

(a) Upon the trial of any such action or proceeding arising out of actions alleged to have been committed by any person arrested for a violation of any paragraph of subdivision two of this section, the court shall admit evidence of the amount of alcohol or drugs in the defendant's blood as shown by a test administered pursuant to the provisions of subdivision seven or eight of this section.

(b) The following effect shall be given to evidence of blood alcohol content, as determined by such tests, of a person arrested for a violation of any paragraph of subdivision two of this section and who was operating a vessel other than a public vessel:

(1) evidence that there was .05 of one per centum or less by weight of alcohol in such person's blood shall be prima facie evidence that the ability of such person to operate a vessel was not impaired by the consumption of alcohol, and that such person was not in an intoxicated condition.

(2) evidence that there was more than .05 of one per centum but less than .07 of one per centum of weight in such person's blood shall be prima facie evidence that such person was not in an intoxicated condition, but such evidence shall be relevant evidence but not be given prima facie effect, in determining whether the ability of such person to operate a vessel was impaired by the consumption of alcohol.

(3) evidence that there was .07 of one per centum or more but less than .08 of one per centum by weight of alcohol in his blood shall be prima facie evidence that such person was not in an intoxicated condition, but such evidence shall be given prima facie effect in determining whether the ability of such person to operate a vessel was impaired by the consumption of alcohol.

(c) Evidence of a refusal to submit to a chemical test or any portion thereof shall be admissible in any trial or hearing provided the request to submit to such a test was made in accordance with the provisions of subdivision seven of this section.

11. Limitations.

(a) A vessel operator may be convicted of a violation of paragraphs (a), (b), (d) and (e) of subdivision two of this section, notwithstanding that the charge laid before the court alleged a violation of paragraph (b), (d) or (e) of subdivision two of this section, and regardless of whether or not such condition is based on a plea of guilty.

(b) In any case wherein the charge laid before the court alleges a violation of paragraph (b), (c), (d) or (e) of subdivision two of this section, any plea of guilty thereafter entered in satisfaction of such charge must include at least a plea of guilty to the violation of the provisions of one of the paragraphs of such subdivision two and no other disposition by plea of guilty to any other charge in satisfaction of such charge shall be authorized; provided, however, if the district attorney upon reviewing the available evidence determines that the charge of a violation of subdivision two of this section is not warranted, he may consent, and the court may allow a disposition by plea of guilty to another charge in satisfaction of such charge.

12. Suspension pending prosecution.

(a) Without notice, pending any prosecution, the court may suspend the right to operate a vessel where the vessel operator has been charged with vehicular assault in the second degree or vehicular manslaughter in the second degree as defined, respectively, in sections 120.03 and 125.12 of the penal law.

(b) A suspension under this subdivision shall occur no later than twenty days after the vessel operator's first appearance before the court on the charges or at the conclusion of all proceedings required for the arraignment, whichever comes first. In order for the court to impose such suspension it must find that the accusatory instrument conforms to the requirements of section 100.40 of the criminal procedure law and there exists reasonable cause to believe that the accused operated a vessel in violation of section 120.03 or 125.12 of the penal law. At such time the operator shall be entitled to an opportunity to make a statement regarding the enumerated issues and to present evidence tending to rebut the court's findings. Where such suspension is imposed upon such pending charge and the operator has requested a hearing pursuant to article one hundred eighty of the criminal procedure law, the court shall conduct such hearing. If upon completion of the hearing, the court fails to find that there is reasonable cause to believe that the operator committed a felony under section 120.03 or 125.12 of the penal law the court shall promptly direct restoration of such operating privileges to the operator unless such operating privileges are suspended or revoked pursuant to any other provision of this chapter.

13. Boating safety course. Upon the conviction of any subdivision of this section, the court shall, in addition to any other penalties invoked under this section, require the convicted person, as a condition of the sentence, to complete a boating safety course of the state, U.S. Power Squadrons, U.S. Coast Guard Auxiliary or a powerboating course or courses offered by the United States sailing association which are approved by the commissioner and show proof of successful completion of such course to the court or its designee.

§ 49-b. Operating a vessel after having consumed alcohol; under the age of twenty-one; per se

1. Prohibition. No person under the age of twenty-one shall operate a vessel upon the waters of this state after having consumed alcohol as defined in this section. For purposes of this section, a person under the age of twenty-one is deemed to have consumed alcohol only if such person has .02 of one per centum or more but not more than .07 of one per centum by weight of alcohol in the person's blood, as shown by chemical analysis of such person's blood, breath, urine or saliva, made in accordance with the provisions of subdivision four of section eleven hundred ninety-four of the vehicle and traffic law. Any person who operates a vessel in violation of this section, and who is not charged with a violation of subdivision two of section forty-nine-a of this article arising out of the same incident shall be referred to the department of motor vehicles for action in accordance with the provisions of this section. Notwithstanding any provision of law to the contrary, a finding that a person under the age of twenty-one operated a vessel after having consumed alcohol in violation of this section is not a judgment of conviction for a crime or any other offense.

2. Breath test for operators of vessel. Every person under the age of twenty-one operating a vessel on the waters of the state which has been involved in an accident or which is operated in violation of any of the provisions of this section or section forty-nine-a of this article which regulate the manner in which a vessel is to be properly operated while underway shall, at the request of a police officer, submit to a breath test to be administered by the police officer. If such test indicates that such operator has consumed alcohol, the police officer may request such operator to submit to a chemical test in the manner set forth in this section. For the purposes of this section, a vessel is being "operated" only when such vessel is underway and is being propelled in whole or in part by mechanical power.

3. Chemical tests.

(a) Any person under the age of twenty-one who operates a vessel on the waters of the state shall be requested to consent to a chemical test of one or more of the following: breath, blood, urine, or saliva for the purpose of determining the alcoholic or drug content of his blood, provided that such test is administered at the direction of a police officer: (1) having reasonable grounds to believe such person to have been operating in violation of this section or paragraph (a), (b), (c), (d) or (e) of subdivision two of section forty-nine-a of this article and within two hours after such person has been placed under arrest, or detained pursuant to paragraph (c) of this subdivision, for any such violation or (2) within two hours after a breath test as provided in subdivision two of this section indicates that alcohol has been consumed by such person and in accordance with the rules and regulations established by the police force of which the officer is a member.

(a-1)If such person having been detained pursuant to paragraph (c) of this subdivision, and having thereafter been requested to submit to such chemical test and having been informed that the person's privilege to operate a vessel and any non-resident operating privilege shall be suspended for refusal to submit to such chemical test or any portion thereof, whether or not there is a finding of operating a vessel after having consumed alcohol, refuses to submit to such chemical test or any portion thereof, unless a court order has been granted pursuant to subdivision eight of section forty-nine-a of this article, the test shall not be given and a written report of such refusal shall be immediately made by the police officer before whom such refusal was made. Such report may be verified by having the report sworn to, or by affixing to such report a form notice that false statements made therein are punishable as a class A misdemeanor pursuant to section 210.45 of the penal law and such form notice together with the subscription of the deponent shall constitute a verification of the report. The report of the police officer shall set forth reasonable grounds to believe such person to have been operating a vessel in violation of this section, and that said person had refused to submit to such chemical test. The report shall be forwarded to the commissioner of motor vehicles within forty-eight hours in a manner to be prescribed by such commissioner of motor vehicles, and all subsequent proceedings with regard to refusal to submit to such chemical test by such person shall be as set forth in subdivision six of this section. The police officer shall provide such person with a hearing date schedule, a waiver form, and such other information as may be required by the commissioner of motor vehicles.

(b) For the purposes of this subdivision, "reasonable grounds" to believe that a person has been operating a vessel after having consumed alcohol in violation of this section shall be determined by viewing the totality of circumstances surrounding the incident which, when taken together, indicate that the operator was operating a vessel in violation of this section. Such circumstances may include any visible or behavioral indication of alcohol consumption by the operator, the existence of an open container containing or having contained an alcoholic beverage in or around the vessel being operated, or any other evidence surrounding the circumstances of the incident which indicates that the operator has been operating a vessel after having consumed alcohol at the time of the incident.

(c) Notwithstanding any other provision of law to the contrary, no person under the age of twenty-one shall be arrested for an alleged violation of this section. However, a person under the age of twenty-one for whom a chemical test is authorized pursuant to this subdivision may be temporarily detained by the police solely for the purpose of requesting or administering such chemical test whenever arrest without a warrant for a petty offense would be authorized in accordance with the provisions of section 140.10 of the criminal procedure law.

4. Chemical test report and hearing.

(a) Whenever a chemical test of the breath, blood, urine or saliva of an operator who is under the age of twenty-one indicates that such person has operated a vessel in violation of this section, and such person is not charged with violating any subdivision of section forty-nine-a of this article arising out of the same incident, the police officer who administered the test shall forward a report of the results of such test to the department of motor vehicles within twenty-four hours of the time when such results are available in a manner prescribed by the commissioner of motor vehicles, and the operator shall be given a hearing notice as provided in subdivision five of this section, to appear before a hearing officer in the county where the chemical test was administered, or in an adjoining county under such circumstances as prescribed by the commissioner of motor vehicles, on a date to be established in accordance with a schedule promulgated by the commissioner of motor vehicles. Such hearing shall occur within thirty days of, but not less than forty-eight hours from, the date that the chemical test was administered, provided, however, where the commissioner of motor vehicles determines, based upon the availability of hearing officers and the anticipated volume of hearings at a particular location, that the scheduling of such hearing within thirty days would impair the timely scheduling or conducting of other hearings, such hearing shall be scheduled at the next hearing date for such particular location. When providing the operator with such hearing notice, the police officer shall also give to the operator, and shall, prior to the commencement of the hearing, provide to the department of motor vehicles, copies of the following reports, documents and materials: any written report or document, or portion thereof, concerning a physical examination, a scientific test or experiment, including the most recent record of inspection, or calibration or repair of machines or instruments utilized to perform such scientific tests or experiments and the certification certificate, if any, held by the operator of the machine or instrument, which tests or examinations were made by or at the request or direction of a public servant engaged in law enforcement activity. The report of the police officer shall be verified by having the report sworn to, or by affixing to such report a form notice that false statements made therein are punishable as a class A misdemeanor pursuant to section 210.45 of the penal law and such form notice together with the subscription of the deponent shall constitute verification of the report.

(b) Every person under the age of twenty-one who is alleged to have operated a vessel after having consumed alcohol as set forth in this section, and who is not charged with violating any subdivision of section forty-nine-a of this article arising out of the same incident, is entitled to a hearing before a hearing officer in accordance with the provisions of this section. Unless otherwise provided by law, the privilege to operate a vessel or any non-resident operating privilege of such person shall not be suspended or revoked prior to the scheduled date for such hearing.

(i) The hearing shall be limited to the following issues: (1) did such person operate the vessel; (2) was a valid request to submit to a chemical test made by the police officer in accordance with the provisions of this section; (3) was such person less than twenty-one years of age at the time of operation of the vessel; (4) was the chemical test properly administered in accordance with the provisions of this section; (5) did the test find that such person had operated a vessel after having consumed alcohol as defined in this section; and (6) did the police officer make a lawful stop of such person. The burden of proof shall be on the police officer to prove each of these issues by clear and convincing evidence.

(ii) Every person who is entitled to a hearing pursuant to this subdivision has the right to be present at the hearing; the right to be represented by attorney, or in the hearing officer's discretion, by any other person the operator chooses; the right to receive and review discovery materials as provided in this subdivision; the right not to testify; the right to present evidence and witnesses in his own behalf, the right to cross examine adverse witnesses, and the right to appeal from an adverse determination in accordance with article three-A of the vehicle and traffic law. Any person representing the operator must conform to the standards of conduct required of attorneys appearing before state courts, and failure to conform to these standards will be grounds for declining to permit his continued appearance in the hearing.

(iii) Hearings conducted pursuant to this subdivision shall be in accordance with this subdivision and with the provisions applicable to the adjudication of traffic infractions pursuant to the following provisions of part 124 of title fifteen of the codes, rules and regulations of the state of New York: paragraph (b) of section 124.1 regarding the opening statement; paragraph (b) of section 124.2 regarding the right to representation and to remain silent and paragraphs (a) through (e) of section 124.4 regarding the conduct of the hearing, procedure and refusal; provided, however, that nothing contained in this subparagraph shall be deemed to preclude a hearing officer from changing the order of a hearing conducted pursuant to this subdivision as justice may require and for good cause shown.

(iv) The rules governing receipt of evidence in a court of law shall not apply in a hearing conducted pursuant to this subdivision except as follows:

(1) on the merits of the charge, and whether or not a party objects, the hearing officer shall exclude from consideration the following: a privileged communication; evidence which, for constitutional reasons, would not be admissible in a court of law; evidence of prior misconduct, incompetency or illness, except where such evidence would be admissible in a

court of law; evidence which is irrelevant or immaterial;

(2) no negative inference shall be drawn from the operator's exercising the right not to testify.

(v) If, after such hearing, the hearing officer, acting on behalf of the commissioner of motor vehicles, finds all of the issues set forth in this subdivision in the affirmative, the hearing officer shall suspend the operating privilege or non-resident operating privilege of such person in accordance with the time periods set forth in this section. If, after such hearing, the hearing officer, acting on behalf of the commissioner of motor vehicles, finds any of said issues in the negative, the hearing officer must find that the operator did not operate a vessel after having consumed alcohol.

(vi) A person who has had a privilege to operate a vessel or non-resident operating privilege suspended pursuant to the provisions of this section may appeal the finding of the hearing officer in accordance with the provisions of article three-A of the vehicle and traffic law.

(c) Unless an adjournment of the hearing date has been granted, upon the operator's failure to appear for a scheduled hearing, the commissioner shall suspend the privilege to operate a vessel or non-resident operating privilege until the operator petitions the commissioner of motor vehicles and a rescheduled hearing is conducted, provided, however, the commissioner shall restore such person's operating privilege or non-resident operating privilege if such rescheduled hearing is adjourned at the request of a person other than the operator. Requests for adjournments shall be made and determined in accordance with regulations promulgated by the commissioner of motor vehicles. If such a request by the operator for an adjournment is granted, the commissioner of motor vehicles shall notify the operator of the rescheduled hearing, which shall be scheduled for the next hearing date. If a second or subsequent request by the operator for an adjournment is granted, the operator's privilege to operate a vessel or, non-resident operating privilege, may be suspended pending the hearing at the time such adjournment is granted; provided, however, that the records of the department or the evidence already admitted furnishes reasonable grounds to believe such suspension is necessary to prevent continuing violations or a substantial safety hazard; and provided further, that such hearing shall be scheduled for the next hearing date.

If a police officer does not appear for a hearing, the hearing officer shall have the authority to dismiss the charge. Any person may waive the right to a hearing under this subdivision, in a form and manner prescribed by the commissioner of motor vehicles, and may enter an admission of guilt, in person or by mail, to the charge of operating a vessel in violation of this section. Such admission of guilt shall have the same force and effect as a finding of guilt entered following a hearing conducted pursuant to this subdivision.

5. Hearing notice. The hearing notice issued to an operator pursuant to subdivision four of this section shall be in a form as prescribed by the commissioner. In addition to containing information concerning the time, date and location of the hearing, and such other information as the commissioner deems appropriate, such hearing notice shall also contain the following information: the date, time and place of the offense charged; the procedures for requesting an adjournment of a scheduled hearing as provided in this section, the operator' s right to a hearing conducted pursuant to this section and the right to waive such hearing and plead guilty, either in person or by mail, to the offense charged.

6. Refusal report and hearing.

(a) Any person under the age of twenty-one who is suspected of operating a vessel after having consumed alcohol in violation of this section, and who is not charged with violating any subdivision of section forty-nine-a of this article arising out of the same incident, and who has been requested to submit to a chemical test pursuant to subdivision three of this section and after having been informed that his privilege to operate a vessel and any non-resident operating privilege shall be suspended for refusal to submit to such chemical test or any portion thereof, whether or not there is a finding of operating a vessel after having consumed alcohol, and such person refuses to submit to such chemical test or any portion thereof, shall be entitled to a hearing in accordance with a schedule promulgated by the commissioner of motor vehicles, and such hearing shall occur within thirty days of, but not less than forty-eight hours from, the date of such refusal, provided, however, where the commissioner of motor vehicles determines, based upon the availability of hearing officers and the anticipated volume of hearings at a particular location, that the scheduling of such hearing within thirty days would impair the timely scheduling or conducting of other hearings, such hearing shall be scheduled at the next hearing date for such particular location.

(b) Unless an adjournment of the hearing date has been granted, upon the operator's failure to appear for a scheduled hearing, the commissioner of motor vehicles shall suspend the operating privilege or non-resident operating privilege until the operator petitions the commissioner of motor vehicles and a rescheduled hearing is conducted, provided, however, the commissioner shall restore such person's operator's privilege or non-resident operating privilege if such rescheduled hearing is adjourned at the request of a person other than the operator. Requests for adjournments shall be made and determined in accordance with regulations promulgated by the commissioner of motor vehicles. If such a request by the operator for an adjournment is granted, the commissioner of motor vehicles shall notify the operator of the rescheduled hearing, which shall be scheduled for the next hearing date. If a second or subsequent request by the operator for an adjournment is granted, the operator's privilege to operate a vessel or non-resident operating privilege may be suspended pending the hearing at the time such adjournment is granted; provided, however, that the records of the department of motor vehicles or the evidence already admitted furnishes reasonable grounds to believe such suspension is necessary to prevent continuing violations or a substantial safety hazard; and provided further, that such hearing shall be scheduled for the next hearing date.

If a police officer does not appear for a hearing, the hearing officer shall have the authority to dismiss the charge. Any person may waive the right to a hearing under this subdivision.

(c) The hearing on the refusal to submit to a chemical test pursuant to this subdivision shall be limited to the following issues: (1) was a valid request to submit to a chemical test made by the police officer in accordance with the provisions of subdivision three of this section; (2) was such person given sufficient warning, in clear or unequivocal language, prior to such refusal that such refusal to submit to such chemical test or any portion thereof, would result in the suspension of such person's privilege to operate a vessel or nonresident operating privilege, whether or not such person is found to have operated a vessel after having consumed alcohol; (3) did such person refuse to submit to such chemical test or any portion thereof; (4) did such person operate the vessel; (5) was such person less than twenty-one years of age at the time of operation of the vessel; (6) did the police officer make a lawful stop of such person. If, after such hearing, the hearing officer, acting on behalf of the commissioner of motor vehicles, finds on any one said issue in the negative, the hearing officer shall not suspend the operator's privilege to operate a vessel or non-resident operating privilege and shall immediately terminate any outstanding suspension of the operator's privilege to operate a vessel or non-resident operating privilege arising from such refusal. If, after such hearing, the hearing officer, acting on behalf of the commissioner of motor vehicles, finds all of the issues in the affirmative, such hearing officer shall immediately suspend the privilege to operate a vessel or any non-resident operating privilege in accordance with the provisions of this section. A person who has had a privilege to operate a vessel or non-resident operating privilege suspended pursuant to the provisions of this section may appeal the findings of the hearing officer in accordance with the provisions of article three-A of the vehicle and traffic law.

(d) Any privilege which has been suspended pursuant to paragraph (c) of this subdivision shall not be restored for one year after such suspension. Where such person under the age of twenty-one years has a prior finding, conviction or youthful offender adjudication resulting from a violation of this section or section forty-nine-a of this article, not arising from the same incident, such privilege shall not be restored for at least one year or until such person reaches the age of twenty-one years, whichever is the greater period of time.

7. Effect of prior finding of having consumed alcohol. A prior finding that a person under the age of twenty-one has operated a vessel after having consumed alcohol pursuant to this section shall have the same effect as a prior conviction of a violation of paragraph (a) of subdivision two of section forty-nine-a of this article solely for the purpose of determining the length of any suspension required to be imposed under any provision of this article, provided that the subsequent offense is committed prior to the expiration of the retention period for such prior offense or offenses set forth in paragraph (k) of subdivision one of section two hundred one of the vehicle and traffic law.

8. Plea bargain limitations.

(a) In any case wherein the charge laid before a court alleges a violation of paragraph (a) of subdivision two of section forty-nine-a of this article and the operator was under the age of twenty-one at the time of such violation, any plea of guilty thereafter entered in satisfaction of such charge must include at least a plea of guilty to the violation of such subdivision; provided, however, such charge may instead be satisfied as provided in paragraph (b) of this subdivision, and, provided further that, if the district attorney, upon reviewing the available evidence, determines that the charge of a violation of paragraph (a) of subdivision two of section forty-nine-a of this article is not warranted, such district attorney may consent, and the court may allow a disposition by plea of guilty to another charge in satisfaction of such charge; provided, however, in all such cases, the court shall set forth upon the record the basis for such disposition.

(b) In any case wherein the charge laid before a court alleges a violation of paragraph (a) of subdivision two of section forty-nine-a of this article by a person who was under the age of twenty-one at the time of commission of the offense, the court, with the consent of both parties, may allow the satisfaction of such charge by the defendant's agreement to be subject to action by the commissioner of motor vehicles pursuant to this section. In any such case, the defendant shall waive the right to a hearing under this section and such waiver shall have the same force and effect as a finding of a violation of this section entered after a hearing conducted pursuant to this section. The defendant shall execute such waiver in open court, and, if represented by counsel, in the presence of his attorney, on a form to be provided by the commissioner of motor vehicles, which shall be forwarded by the court to the commissioner of motor vehicles within ninety-six hours. To be valid, such form shall, at a minimum, contain clear and conspicuous language advising the defendant that a duly executed waiver: (i) has the same force and effect as a guilty finding following a hearing pursuant to this section; (ii) shall subject the defendant to the imposition of sanctions pursuant to this section; and (iii) may subject the defendant to increased sanctions upon a subsequent violation of this section or section forty-nine-a of this article. Upon receipt of a duly executed waiver pursuant to this paragraph, the commissioner of motor vehicles shall take such administrative action and impose such sanctions as may be required by this section.

9. Sanctions.

(a) Except as otherwise provided in this subdivision, a person's privilege to operate a vessel upon the waters of the state shall be suspended for six months, where such person has been found to have operated a vessel after having consumed alcohol in violation of this section.

(b) The suspension of operating privileges pursuant to this subdivision shall be for one year or until such person reaches the age of twenty-one, whichever is the greater period of time, where such person has been found to have operated a vessel after having consumed alcohol in violation of this section, and has previously been found to have operated a vessel after having consumed alcohol in violation of this section or has previously been convicted of, or adjudicated a youthful offender for any violation of section forty-nine-a of this article not arising out of the same incident.

(c) Where the commissioner of motor vehicles determines that the period of suspension imposed pursuant to this section would extend beyond the current boating season, such commissioner may direct that any portion of such suspension period take effect during the following boating season.

10. Civil penalty.

(a) Unless otherwise provided, any person whose privilege to operate a vessel has been suspended pursuant to the provisions of this section shall also be liable for a civil penalty in the amount of one hundred twenty-five dollars.

(b) The first one hundred dollars of each civil penalty collected pursuant to the provisions of this section shall be paid to the commissioner of motor vehicles for deposit into the general fund and the remainder of all such civil penalties shall be paid to the commissioner of parks, recreation, and historic preservation for deposit into the "I Love NY Waterways" boating safety fund established pursuant to section ninety-seven-nn of state finance law.

11. Nothing contained in this section shall be deemed to exempt persons under the age of twenty-one from arrest and prosecution under section forty-nine-a of this article for an alleged violation of such section.

§ 49-c. Termination of unsafe operation

A police officer or peace officer, acting pursuant to his or her special duties, who has reasonable cause to believe that a vessel, including a rowboat, canoe or kayak, is being operated, in his or her presence, upon the navigable waters of the state, or any tidewaters bordering on or lying within the boundaries of the county of Nassau or Suffolk, in violation of any section of this article, and that it would be so imminently hazardous to continue to operate such vessel as to be likely to cause an accident or physical injury, may direct the master or operator of such vessel to cease operating upon such waters, and to proceed immediately to dock the vessel at the nearest available safe anchorage, dock or mooring until the violation charged by such officer is finally adjudicated or until such hazardous condition is remediated or otherwise corrected.

Part 2 Public Vessels

§ 50. Owners to notify inspector and apply for inspection

It shall be the duty of the owner of a public vessel which he intends to operate on the navigable waters of the state to notify the inspector of such intention at least one month before it is desired to place the vessel in operation and to request an inspection of such vessel. Upon receipt of such notification the inspector shall enter the application on the records of his office. A temporary permit to operate such vessel pending inspection may be issued by the inspector, if he finds through documentary evidence that such vessel is properly equipped and manned for the safety of life and property. No public vessel shall be used or operated without a certificate of inspection or a temporary permit as herein provided.

§§ 51, 52. [Repealed]

§ 53. Rules and regulations

The commissioner may adopt, amend and repeal rules and regulations as he or she deems necessary to carry out the provisions of this part.

§ 54. Construction against fire

All public vessels shall be so constructed that inflammable material about any machinery or apparatus involving danger of fire where such inflammable material is exposed to ignition, shall be shielded by some incombustible material so that the air may circulate freely between such material and the ignitable substances. Before granting a certificate of inspection, the inspector shall require that all necessary provisions be made throughout such vessel as he may judge expedient to guard against loss or damage by fire.

§ 55. Stairways and passageways

1. Every public vessel certified to carry passengers shall be provided with (a) permanent

stairways and other sufficient and safe means convenient for passing from one deck to the other, and (b) passageways large enough to allow persons freely to pass, which shall be open fore and aft of the length of the vessel, and to and along the railings, which shall be functional, unobstructed and passable whenever the vessel is engaged in carrying passengers.

2. In addition to any other requirement imposed by this section, public vessels certified to carry more than twenty passengers shall be provided with a minimum of two means of egress on each deck which shall be functional, unobstructed and passable whenever the vessel is engaged in carrying passengers.

3. Any person who operates a public vessel, and any owner of a public vessel who permits a person to operate such vessel, in contravention of the requirements of subdivision one of this section, shall be guilty of a violation punishable as set forth in section seventy-three-c of this article.

4. Any person who operates a public vessel, and any owner of a public vessel who permits a person to operate such vessel, in contravention of the requirements of subdivision two of this section, shall be guilty of a misdemeanor punishable as set forth in section seventy-three-b of this article.

5. The license of any master, pilot, engineer, or joint pilot and engineer who operates a public vessel in contravention of any of the requirements of this section may be subject to the suspension or revocation of his or her license pursuant to section sixty-four-a of this article.

§ 56. Fire pump

Every public vessel permitted by her certificate to carry one hundred passengers or more, shall be provided with a fire pump or other equivalent apparatus for throwing water, the same to be at all times during the navigation of such vessel, kept ready for immediate use, having hose of suitable size and sufficient strength to stand a pressure of at least seventy-five pounds to the square inch, and of a length to be specified by the inspector. The inspector may require the installation of an approved fixed fire extinguishing system as defined in subdivision five of section sixty-seven in lieu of, or in addition to, the fire pump required by this section.

§ 57. Identification number of vessel

Every public vessel subject to the provisions of this chapter shall be registered and display the identification number assigned as set forth in section twenty-two hundred fifty-one of the vehicle and traffic law. In addition to the number assigned, each public vessel shall display the letters "PV" not more than six inches above or below the identification number. The letters "PV" shall be not less than five inches in height and maintained in a legible condition so that the letters, "PV", are readily discernible during daylight hours at a distance of two hundred feet. It shall be the duty of every owner to register and display numbers as herein indicated. Violation of this section shall be a violation punishable by a fine of not less than twenty-five nor more than one hundred dollars.

§ 58. Number of passengers

It shall not be lawful to take on board of any public vessel a greater number of passengers than the number allowed in the certificate of inspection and for every violation of this provision, the master, pilot, joint pilot and engineer or owner shall be guilty of a misdemeanor punishable as set forth in section seventy-three-b of this article.

§ 58-a. Unauthorized boarding of vessels

(1) It shall be unlawful for any person except a pilot or public officer to board or attempt to board, a vessel arriving in the port of New York before such vessel shall have been made fast to the wharf, without first obtaining leave from the master or person having charge of such vessel, or leave in writing from her owners or agents.

(2) It shall be unlawful for any person to board or attempt to board any vessel arriving in or lying or being in the port of New York, with intent to supply liquors by sale, gift or otherwise, directly or indirectly, to any member of the crew employed on board of such vessel.

(3) It shall be unlawful for any person having boarded any vessel in the port of New York, to neglect or refuse to leave such vessel after having been ordered to do so by the master or person in charge of such vessel.

(4) The word "vessel" as used in this section shall include vessels by whatever power propelled.

(5) Any person violating any of the provisions of this section shall be deemed guilty of a

misdemeanor punishable as set forth in section seventy-three-b of this article.

§ 59. Manning of public vessels

1. All public vessels while under way under their own power, shall be in charge of a licensed master, pilot, engineer, or joint pilot and engineer. Anyone operating a public vessel without a license and any owner who permits the operation of a public vessel by a person who does not possess a valid license or temporary permit, in full force and effect as master, pilot, engineer or joint pilot and engineer shall be guilty of a misdemeanor punishable as set forth in section seventy-three-b of this article.

2. It shall be unlawful to operate a public vessel with less than the required crew members as specified in the certificate of inspection or temporary permit. Any person who operates a public vessel, and any owner of a public vessel who permits a person to operate such vessel, in contravention of this requirement, shall be guilty of a misdemeanor punishable as set forth in section seventy-three-b of this article. In addition, the license of any master, pilot, engineer, or joint pilot and engineer who operates a public vessel in contravention of the crew requirements as contained in the certificate of inspection may be subject to the suspension or revocation of his or her license pursuant to section sixty-four-a of this article.

§ 60. Inability to provide licensed officer

If the owner or master of a public vessel is unable to obtain the services of a licensed officer, the inspector shall be notified and the deficiency may be temporarily supplied, if the inspector approves, until the services of a licensed officer can be obtained.

§ 61. Repairs and modifications

1. Before any repair or modification is made to the structure or engineering plant of a public vessel, or any repair or modification is made that may affect the stability, seaworthiness or safe operation of a public vessel, or in the event that the owner of a public vessel becomes aware of any such repair or modification, the owner shall notify the inspector of the repair or modification or proposed repair or modification in writing. The inspector shall be authorized to determine whether a proposed repair or modification may be made, whether inspection of the vessel shall be required before any proposed repair or modification is made, or whether inspection should be made after repair or modification. The inspector shall also be authorized to determine whether the vessel may be operated

pending inspection, or whether the vessel may only be operated after inspection, or whether it may not be operated. The inspector may impose conditions on any such repair or modification, inspection and operation taking into consideration the nature of the proposed or existing repair or modification, the condition of the vessel and any other factors the inspector deems relevant to the stability, seaworthiness and safe operation of such vessel. The owner shall comply with the determination of the inspector.

2. An owner who fails to give notification as required by this section, or who modifies or permits the repair or modification of a public vessel in contravention of the requirements of this section, shall be guilty of a violation punishable as set forth in section seventy-three-c of this article.

3. A public vessel which the inspector has directed to be inspected prior to operation pursuant to the provisions of this section shall not be operated upon the navigable waters of the state if such vessel has not been inspected. A public vessel which the inspector has directed not to be operated pursuant to the provisions of this section shall not be operated upon the navigable waters of the state. An owner who permits the operation of a public vessel in contravention of this section shall be guilty of a misdemeanor punishable as set forth in [section]* seventy-three-b of this article, and the certificate of inspection of said public vessel may, in the discretion of the inspector, be suspended until such time as the inspector determines that said vessel is stable, seaworthy and safe.

§ 62. Loss of life by misconduct of officers

Every master or other person employed on any public vessel, by whose misconduct, negligence or inattention to his or her duties on such vessel, the life of any person is lost, and every owner or charterer through whose fraud, neglect, misconduct or violation of law, the life of any person is lost, shall be guilty of a class E felony.

§ 63. Certificate of inspection

The inspector, if satisfied that a public vessel is in all respects safe and conforms to the requirement of this chapter, shall make and subscribe duplicate certificates setting forth the name and number of the vessel, its age, the date of inspection, the name of the owner, the number of licensed officers and crew necessary to manage the vessel with safety, equipment required and any special restrictions or remarks pertaining to the operation of the vessel and the number of passengers she can safely carry, and, if a steam vessel, the age of the boiler and the pressure of steam she is authorized to carry. One of said certificates shall be kept posted in some conspicuous place on the vessel to be designated by the inspector and the other copy shall be kept by the inspector and by him recorded in a book to be kept for that purpose. If the inspector refuses to grant a certificate of approval, he shall make a statement in writing, giving his reasons for such refusal, and deliver the same to the owner or master of the vessel. The posting of certificates of inspection shall not be required on vessels of less than ten tons burden. However said certificates must be aboard whenever the vessel is in operation.

§ 64. Licenses

Every person employed as a master, pilot, engineer or joint pilot and engineer, on board of a public vessel, shall be examined by the inspector as to his qualifications, and if the inspector is satisfied therewith, he shall grant him a license for the term of one year. In a proper case, the license may permit and specify that the master may act as pilot, and in case of small vessels may also act as joint pilot and engineer. The license shall be framed under glass and posted in some conspicuous place on the vessel on which he may act, provided that on vessels of less than ten tons, the license must be carried but need not be posted. Whoever acts as master, pilot, engineer, or joint pilot and engineer, without having first received such license, except as in this article otherwise specified, shall be guilty of a misdemeanor. An applicant for license as master, pilot, or engineer, must be at least twenty-one years of age. An applicant for a license as joint pilot and engineer must be at least eighteen years of age.

§ 64-a. Suspension and revocation of licenses

1. The inspector may suspend or revoke any license of master, pilot, engineer or joint pilot and engineer, issued pursuant to the provisions of this article, upon satisfactory proof of recklessness, carelessness, intemperance, incompetence, wilful dereliction of duty or wilful disobedience of any rule or regulation duly made and promulgated by the commissioner.

2. It shall be the duty of the inspector to receive and make determination on complaints duly made in writing against any master, pilot, engineer, or joint pilot and engineer licensed pursuant to the provisions of this article where it appears that the license of such person may be subject to suspension or revocation under this section.

3. Before any person shall be proceeded against on any complaint and before any license may be revoked or suspended, such person shall be notified, in writing, signed by the inspector, to appear before the inspector. Such notice shall specify the nature and substance of such complaint and shall be served personally at least five days before the time fixed for appearance. The inspector may postpone or adjourn such hearing from time to time.

4. The inspector, at the request of either the complaining or defending party, shall issue subpoenas to compel the attendance of witnesses before the inspector in all cases which he is empowered to hear and determine under this article. The inspector shall examine on oath, to be administered by him, all such witnesses. Each person subpoenaed as a witness shall be entitled to the same witness fees and be subject to the same penalties and punishments for disobedience, or for false testimony, as would apply in a civil suit at law, in a court of record.

5. Whenever the license of any master, pilot, engineer or joint pilot and engineer is suspended or revoked he shall forthwith deliver up his license to the inspector. The inspector shall retain any such suspended license until the time of suspension shall expire. Any such person who shall refuse to deliver up such suspended or revoked license shall be subject to a penalty of one hundred dollars for each day following such refusal.

§ 65. Fees for vessel inspections and for the issuance of licenses

The owner of a public vessel, inspected and licensed as provided in this chapter, shall pay to the inspector, for each vessel not over ten tons burden, twenty dollars; for each vessel over ten and not over twenty tons burden, thirty dollars; for each vessel over twenty and not over fifty tons burden, forty dollars; for each vessel over fifty and not over one hundred tons burden, fifty dollars; and for each vessel over one hundred tons burden, one hundred dollars. Each person licensed, as provided for in this chapter, shall pay twenty dollars for each original license and ten dollars for each renewal thereof. All moneys received by the office for examinations, licenses or renewals of licenses, shall be deposited into the "I love NY waterways" boating safety fund established pursuant to section ninety-seven-nn of the state finance law.

§ 66. Inflammable or explosive articles prohibited

1. No loose hay, loose cotton, or loose hemp, camphene, nitro-glycerine, naptha

[naphtha]*, benzine, benzol, coal-oil, crude petroleum or other like explosive burning fluids or dangerous articles, shall be carried as freight or used as stores on any public vessel carrying passengers licensed under this chapter, except that refined petroleum which will not ignite at a temperature of less than one hundred and ten degrees Fahrenheit may be carried on the main deck of any public vessel, provided the barrels or cases containing such oil are fully covered with a tarpaulin. But nothing in this section shall be construed to prevent any vessel utilizing petroleum, petroleum products or other mineral oils as a source of motive power, from carrying for its own use, in reasonable quantities, petroleum, petroleum products and oils in metal tanks, properly protected, vented and located, such tanks, their piping, equipment and manner of installation to be subject to the approval of the inspector, and such approval when given shall be indorsed on the certificate of inspection issued to such vessel, nor shall the provisions of this section prohibit the transportation by vessels of gasoline or other petroleum products when carried in the tanks of motor vehicles using gasoline or petroleum products as a source of motive power, provided that all fire in such vehicles shall be extinguished and their engines and motors stopped immediately after boarding such vessels, and no fire shall be lighted nor the engine or motor of such vehicle shall be started until immediately before such vehicle shall leave the vessel.

2. It shall be unlawful for the operator of any marina providing facilities for sale of fuel to vessels, to maintain fuel pumps on the premises unless equipped as may be necessary for the arresting of static electricity. All motors and generators on the vessel being refueled shall be turned off during the refueling process.

A violation of the provisions of this section shall constitute a violation punishable as set forth in section seventy-three-c of this article.

§ 67. Public vessel equipment

1. Buoyant apparatus. Every public vessel of over fifty tons burden, navigating more than one mile from shore, shall carry in addition to other equipment required by this section, sufficient buoyant apparatus for not less than twenty per cent of all persons on board. Buoyant apparatus shall mean and include life rafts, or life floats, of a type approved by the commissioner. Such apparatus shall be equipped with oars or paddles and other equipment as specified by the inspector. All buoyant apparatus shall be stowed in such a manner that

it is easily accessible and capable of being launched into the waters in case of need.

2. Personal flotation devices. Every public vessel engaged in the transportation of passengers shall have on board a wearable personal flotation device for each passenger the vessel is certified to carry, and one additional wearable personal flotation device for each member of the crew. The personal flotation devices shall be of a type approved by the United States coast guard for use on vessels carrying passengers for hire. The personal flotation devices shall be in serviceable condition and kept in readily accessible places, having the approval of the inspector, for immediate use in case of emergency. The location of the personal flotation devices shall be indicated by legible printed notices. It shall be the duty of the inspector to ascertain that every personal flotation device is as herein required.

3. Ventilation. The inspector shall require that machinery and other enclosed spaces be adequately ventilated by means of free or forced air ventilation. The inspector shall require that all installed fuel tanks be properly vented.

4. Portable fire extinguishers. The inspector shall require that public vessels carry such portable fire extinguishers as he deems necessary and to specify their type, size and location on the vessel, dependent upon the type of vessel, the number of passengers and the amount and character of freight carried and other fire hazards.

5. Fixed fire extinguishing systems. Fixed fire extinguishing systems, hereinafter termed "fixed systems", are considered to be total flooding systems using carbon dioxide as the extinguishing agent and having components fixed in position. The inspector shall require the installation of a fixed system on every passenger carrying public vessel which has enclosed engine and fuel tank compartments.

6. Communications and navigational equipment. Every public vessel certified to carry more than ten passengers shall be equipped with either a very high frequency marine radio or operational cellular phone which, considering the location of the vessel's operations, the vessel's range, the availability of persons or services to receive and respond to the vessel's transmissions when the vessel is in use and other relevant factors the inspector, in his or her discretion, determines to be a reliable means for such vessel to call for any necessary aid or assistance. Every public vessel certified to carry more than sixty-five passengers shall also be equipped with functional radar.

7. Marking of equipment. All equipment, unless otherwise directed by the inspector, shall be legibly marked with the name or registration number of the public vessel on which it is carried.

8. The commissioner is hereby authorized to make rules and regulations pertaining to equipment on public vessels. In framing such rules and regulations the commissioner shall, as far as practicable, be governed by the rules and regulations of the United States coast guard prescribed for the regulation of commercial vessels.

§ 68. Investigations by inspector; penalties; reports

The inspector upon order or pursuant to direction of the commissioner shall investigate all violations and charges of violations of the provisions of this article which are applicable to public vessels. Should the investigations disclose that a person has sustained bodily injury through accident caused as the direct result of any such violation, he shall file with the district attorney of the county in which such violation occurred, a statement of the nature of the violation, the injury sustained and the names of the persons involved and of the witnesses thereto. Any master, owner, or other person violating any of such provisions, in addition to any other punishment prescribed by this chapter or other law, shall forfeit to the people of the state a sum of not less than twenty-five nor more than one hundred dollars to be fixed by the court or justice for each and every offense; every violation shall be a separate and distinct offense, and, in case of a continuing violation, every day's continuance thereof shall be deemed to be a separate and distinct offense.

§ 69. Seizure of public vessels

Whenever the inspector shall find after investigation or have reasonable cause to believe that any public vessel is being operated in contravention of the provisions of this article, or is being operated by an unlicensed person by and with the consent of the owner, he may seize and impound such vessel until the termination of the action against the owner to recover the penalty therefor and thereafter until the penalty imposed by the court or justice has been paid. Such seizure and impoundment of any public vessel by the inspector shall be at the owner's risk. Within fifteen days after the entry of judgment by the court or justice, the inspector may, unless the judgment be sooner paid and in lieu of proceeding by body execution, sell the public vessel so impounded at public sale upon notice to the owner.

Notice of the sale, specifying the date, place and hour of the sale shall be served upon the owner of the public vessel personally or by registered mail addressed to him at his last known post-office address, and published not less than ten days before the sale. The publication of notice of sale shall be made in a newspaper or newspapers designated by the commissioner having general circulation in the county where the public vessel was seized and impounded. The proceeds of sale shall first be applied in payment of the judgment and expenses of sale and the remainder shall be paid to the owner of the public vessel or other person lawfully entitled thereto. If the commissioner is unable to determine by reasonable investigation the person or persons entitled to the remainder of the proceeds of sale, he may deposit the same with the supreme court in the third judicial district for final determination thereon.

Part 2-A Petroleum-Bearing Vessels

§ 70. Minimum conditions for petroleum-bearing vessels in certain areas; tanker-avoidance zones

1. The commissioner of environmental conservation in consultation with the petroleum-bearing vessel advisory commission established in section seventy-one of this article, the United States Coast Guard, the board of commissioners of pilots and appropriate officials of any state or country with concurrent jurisdiction over water bodies which might be affected, through rule and regulation may establish standards setting forth:

(a) the minimum conditions under which petroleum-bearing vessels as defined in section one hundred seventy-two of this chapter may enter or move upon the navigable waters of the state and any tidewaters bordering on or lying within the boundaries of Nassau and Suffolk counties. Such conditions may include, but not be limited to, visibility, the tide and wind conditions and weather; and

(b) the minimum conditions under which petroleum-bearing vessels may enter or leave any major facility, port or harbor. Such conditions may include, but not be limited to, visibility, the tide and wind conditions and weather.

2. The commissioner of environmental conservation may, in consultation with the petroleum-bearing vessel advisory commission established in section seventy-one of this article, the United States Coast Guard, the board of commissioners of pilots and appropriate

officials of any state or country with concurrent jurisdiction over water bodies which might be affected, establish tanker-avoidance zones, where it shall be unlawful for petroleum-bearing vessels as defined in section one hundred seventy-two of this chapter, to enter or move upon the navigable waters of the state or any tidewaters bordering on or lying within the boundaries of Nassau and Suffolk counties.

§ 70-a. Minimum conditions for petroleum-bearing vessels on the Hudson river; tanker-avoidance zones

1. The commissioner of environmental conservation in consultation with the United States Coast Guard, the board of commissioners of pilots, the department of state, at least one licensed Hudson river pilot and appropriate officials of any state which might be affected, may establish guidelines setting forth:

(a) the minimum conditions under which petroleum-bearing vessels as defined in section one hundred seventy-two of this chapter may enter or move upon the navigable waters of the Hudson river. Such conditions may include, but not be limited to: (i) visibility; (ii) the tide and wind conditions; and (iii) weather;

(b) the minimum conditions under which petroleum-bearing vessels may enter or leave any major facility, port or harbor along the Hudson river. Such conditions may include, but are not be limited to: (i) visibility; (ii) the tide and wind conditions; and (iii) weather;

(c) the establishment of tanker-avoidance zones, where it shall be unlawful for petroleum-bearing vessels as defined in section one hundred seventy-two of this chapter, to enter, move or anchor upon the navigable waters of the Hudson river, except in cases of great emergency. Such tanker-avoidance zones may be based upon physical and environmental conditions which may include, but are not limited to: (i) navigational hazards; (ii) environmental conditions; (iii) the existence of designated significant coastal fish and wildlife habitats; (iv) proximity to waterfront communities; (v) disproportionate impacts on communities; and (vi) federally or state identified environmental remediation sites; and may consider an affected community's waterfront revitalization plan or comprehensive plan and the environmental justice communities impacts.

2. The commissioner of environmental conservation following consultation with the United States Coast Guard, the board of commissioners of pilots, the department of state, the office

of parks, recreation and historic preservation, at least one licensed Hudson river pilot and appropriate officials of any state which might be affected, shall submit a report to the governor, the temporary president of the senate, and the speaker of the assembly within one hundred twenty days of the effective date of this section regarding recommendations on plans, policies and programs affecting petroleum-bearing vessels on the navigable waters of the Hudson river, as well as on any proposed rulemaking from the United States Coast Guard which would impact the Hudson river.

§ 71. Petroleum-bearing vessel advisory commission

1. Creation of the petroleum-bearing vessel advisory commission. The commissioner of environmental conservation shall establish a petroleum-bearing vessel advisory commission to make recommendations on plans, policies and programs affecting petroleum-bearing vessels. Such advisory commission shall be composed of nine members to be appointed by the commissioner. The chairperson shall be designated by the commissioner of environmental conservation. All members of the commission shall have knowledge of and experience in the pilotage of commercial vessels. At least three members shall be licensed pilots by the state of New York, and at least two members shall be pilots licensed by states contiguous to New York or by Canada and at least two members shall be experienced in the navigation and pilotage of tug boats and petroleum-bearing barges. Appointments to the advisory commission shall be made no later than the first day of January next succeeding the date on which this section will have become a law.

2. Meetings of the advisory commission. The advisory commission shall meet at least annually.

3. Duties of the advisory commission. The advisory commission shall have the following powers and duties:

(a) to advise the commissioner of environmental conservation in establishing minimum conditions for petroleum-bearing vessels in certain waters, pursuant to section seventy of this article.

(b) to advise the commissioner of environmental conservation in establishing tanker-avoidance zones, pursuant to section seventy of this article.

4. Term of appointment. All members of the advisory commission shall serve terms of three

years.

5. State assistance. The commissioner of environmental conservation and all state agencies shall make any and all documents readily available to the advisory commission which are needed to properly and thoroughly carry out its responsibilities. The commissioner of environmental conservation shall also make available to the advisory commission such staff assistance reasonably necessary to allow the advisory commission to carry out its duties and responsibilities.

Part 3 Pleasure Vessels

§§ 71, 71b. [Repealed]

§ 71-c. [Repealed]

§ 71-d. Liveries; safety regulations; penalty

1. No livery operator shall knowingly lease, hire or rent a vessel to any person:

(a) When the number of persons using the vessel shall exceed the number deemed to constitute a maximum safety load for said vessel, according to its capacity plate or industry-accepted standards.

(b) When the manufacturer's rated horsepower of the motor exceeds the capacity of the vessel, making the vessel unsafe to operate.

(c) When the vessel does not contain the equipment required by its respective class, as provided by section forty.

1-a. Notwithstanding subdivision one of section forty-nine of this article, a livery may lease, hire or rent a mechanically propelled vessel, except a personal water craft or specialty prop craft, to a person who is not the holder of a boating safety certificate if:

(a) the person is eighteen years or older;

(b) the operator of such livery or his or her designated agent, is the holder of a boating safety certificate, and prior to permitting the use by such person of the vessel explains and demonstrates to such person by video or actual in water demonstration the operation of such vessel, and the use and location of such vessel's safety equipment;

(c) such person, after receiving the explanation and demonstration required pursuant to paragraph (b) of this subdivision, demonstrates to the livery operator or the livery operator's designated agent the ability to operate such vessel and use the applicable safety equipment;

(d) such person presents genuine proof of identification and age to the livery operator;

(e) the livery operator or the livery operator's designated agent, at the time of the leasing, hiring, or renting, records the name, address, and age of the operator of the leased, hired or rented vessel. Such records shall be maintained for a period of not less than one year; and

(f) the vessel is not leased, hired or rented to the same person for a period exceeding sixty days.

2. Any person convicted of violating this section shall be guilty of a violation punishable by a fine of not less than twenty-five nor more than one hundred dollars.

§ 72. Operation of pleasure vessels on Round Island lake, Orange county

Pleasure vessels as defined in this chapter, equipped with detachable outboard motors or permanent inboard motors, except vessels propelled by electric motors of not over one-fourth rated horsepower, shall not be operated at any time on the waters of Round Island lake, Orange county.

§ 72-a. Operation of vessels on the inland waters of Chautauqua county

No water craft shall pass the stern of a boat being used for trolling less than two hundred feet from the stern of such boat on the inland lakes of Chautauqua county.

§ 73. Towing of persons

1. No person shall operate a vessel for towing a person unless there is upon such vessel a person, other than the operator, of at least ten years of age, in a position to observe the progress of the person being towed.

2. No person shall be towed or use or operate a vessel to tow a person during the period from sunset to sunrise provided, however, that the provisions of this subdivision shall not apply to a paid performer engaged in a professional exhibition.

3. No person shall be towed by a vessel without wearing a securely fastened United States Coast Guard approved personal flotation device and no person shall use or operate a vessel to tow a person not in compliance with this subdivision; provided, however, that the provisions of this subdivision shall not apply to a paid performer engaged in a professional exhibition.

4. The provisions of subdivision one of this section shall not apply to a vessel operated or controlled by the person being towed by such vessel, the design of which makes no provision for carrying an operator or observer on board. Such a vessel may not, however, be operated unless (a) it is registered and an assigned number permanently displayed thereon in accordance with sections twenty-two hundred fifty-one and twenty-two hundred fifty-four of the vehicle and traffic law; (b) it is equipped with an automatic shut-off mechanism activated whenever the operator is separated from the towing device; (c) it is equipped with a fire extinguisher and flame arrester attached to the motor; (d) the motor compartment is properly ventilated; (e) all persons being towed are wearing a securely fastened United States Coast Guard approved personal flotation device at all times of operation; and (f) other safety provisions required by section forty of this article, except the requirements of subdivisions two and three thereof relating to the use of whistles and anchors.

4-a. No person shall operate or manipulate any vessel or device for towing a person in such a way as to cause such device or any person utilizing such device to collide with or strike any object or person. The provisions of this section do not apply to collisions of two or more persons or devices being towed behind the same boat nor to collisions with ski jumps, buoys and similar objects normally used in competitive or recreational water skiing.

5. No person shall operate or manipulate a device for towing a person or be towed in a reckless or negligent manner so as to endanger the life, limb, or property of any person.

6. Any person violating any provision of this section shall be guilty of a violation punishable as set forth in section seventy-three-c of this article.

7. For the purposes of this section: (a) to tow a person shall mean the towing of a person, including utilizing a device, on the navigable waters of the state or any tidewaters bordering on or lying within the boundaries of Nassau and Suffolk counties, but shall not include the towing of persons in a vessel to which assistance is being rendered; and (b) a device shall include, but not be limited to, water skis, a tube, a surfboard, a tow rope, an aquaplane, a parasail, or a related device.

§ 73-a. Regulations of personal watercraft and specialty prop-craft

1. Personal watercraft and specialty prop-craft.

a. No person shall operate a personal watercraft or a specialty prop-craft unless each person riding on such vessel is wearing a securely fastened United States Coast Guard approved personal flotation device.

b. No person shall operate a personal watercraft or a specialty prop-craft unless such vessel is equipped and fitted with a United States Coast Guard approved device for arresting carburetor backfire.

c. No person shall operate a personal watercraft or a specialty prop-craft unless such vessel is equipped with:

(i) at least two ventilators fitted with cowls or their equivalent for the purpose of properly and efficiently ventilating the bilges of every engine and fuel tank compartment in order to remove any inflammable or explosive gases provided, however, if the vessel is so constructed as to have the greater portion of the bilges under the engine and fuel tanks open and exposed to the natural atmosphere at all times such vessel need not be required to be fitted with such ventilators; and

(ii) an efficient sound producing mechanical appliance, except sirens, capable of producing a blast of two seconds or more in duration and of such strength as to be heard plainly for a distance of at least one-half mile in still weather; and

(iii) a fluorescent-orange distress flag which shall be a minimum of one foot square or other appropriate United States Coast Guard approved visual distress signal.

d. Any person operating a personal watercraft or a specialty prop-craft equipped by the manufacturer with a lanyard type engine cut-off switch shall attach such lanyard to his or her person, clothing, or personal flotation device as is appropriate for the specific vessel.

e. No person shall operate a personal watercraft or a specialty prop-craft at any time from sunset to sunrise.

f. No person shall operate a personal watercraft or a specialty prop-craft within five hundred feet of any designated bathing area, except in bodies of water where the opposing shoreline is less than five hundred feet from such designated area and in accordance with speed regulations and restrictions as provided by local law or ordinance but in no event at a speed in excess of ten miles per hour, provided, however, that nothing contained in this subdivision shall be construed to prohibit the launching of such vessel from designated launching areas or sites.

g. Every personal watercraft and specialty prop-craft shall at all times be operated in a reasonable and prudent manner. Maneuvers which unreasonably or unnecessarily endanger life, limb, or property, including, but not limited to, (i) weaving through congested vessel traffic, or (ii) jumping the wake of another vessel unreasonably or unnecessarily close to such other vessel or when visibility around such other vessel is obstructed, or (iii) swerving at the last possible moment to avoid collision shall constitute reckless operation of a vessel, as provided in section forty-five of this article.

h. The provisions of this section shall not apply to any performer engaged in a professional exhibition or any person preparing to participate or participating in a regatta, race, marine parade, tournament, or exhibition authorized under section thirty-four of this chapter.

i. The provisions of this section shall apply to the operation of a personal watercraft and a specialty prop-craft on any waterway or body of water located within New York state and not privately owned and any part of any body of water adjacent to New York state over which the state has territorial jurisdiction, including all tidewaters bordering on and lying within the boundaries of Nassau and Suffolk counties.

j. The provisions of section forty of this chapter shall not apply to personal watercraft or specialty prop-craft.

2. Liveries. Notwithstanding the provisions of section forty-nine or seventy-one-d of this chapter, no livery shall lease, hire, or rent a personal watercraft or a specialty prop-craft to any person unless:

(a) such person is sixteen years of age or older.

(b) the operator of such livery, or his designated agent, prior to permitting the use by such person of such personal watercraft or specialty prop-craft, explains and demonstrates to such person by video or actual in water demonstration the operating procedure of such personal watercraft or specialty prop-craft and the use of such vessel's safety equipment;

(c) such person, after receiving the explanation and demonstration required pursuant to paragraph (b) of this subdivision, demonstrates to such livery operator or to such designated agent the ability to operate such vessel and use the applicable safety equipment;

(d) such person has presented genuine proof of identification and age; and except as provided in paragraph (f) of this subdivision, has demonstrated compliance with section forty-nine of this article, to such livery operator or the livery operator's designated agent prior to the time of leasing, hiring or renting such vessel;

(e) such livery operator or his designated agent, at the time of such leasing, hiring or renting, records the name, address and age of the user of the leased, hired or rented vessel, and the model, year, name of manufacturer, and state registration or federal documentation numbers of the leased, hired or rented vessel. Such records shall be maintained for a period of not less than one year; and

(f) [Expires and repealed Jan 1, 2021] notwithstanding the provisions of paragraph (d) of this subdivision and subdivision one-a of section forty-nine of this article, a person over eighteen years of age may operate such personal watercraft or specialty prop-craft without the certificate required pursuant to section forty-nine of this article when such operation is restricted by the operator of such livery, or the livery operator's designated agent, to a specified area, no part of which shall be more than twenty-five hundred feet from the livery location, or, if removed from the livery location, not more than five hundred feet from the livery operator or agent assigned by the livery operator to supervise such operation and such personal watercraft or specialty propcraft and/or the personal flotation device of the operator is clearly marked in such a manner as to be distinguishable by the operator of such livery or the livery operator's designated agent within the permitted areas of operation.

3. Penalties for violation.

(a) Every person convicted of a violation of this section, other than a conviction for a violation of subdivision two of this section, shall for a first conviction thereof be punished by a fine of not less than fifty dollars nor more than two hundred dollars; for a conviction of a second violation, both of which were committed within a period of twenty-four months, such person shall be punished by a fine of not less than one hundred dollars nor more than four hundred dollars; upon a conviction of a third or subsequent violation, all of which were committed within a period of twenty-four months, such person shall be punished by a fine of not less than two hundred dollars nor more than five hundred dollars and the revocation of the registration of the personal watercraft.

(b) Every person convicted of a violation of subdivision two of this section shall for a first conviction thereof be punished by a fine of not less than one hundred dollars nor more than two hundred dollars; for a conviction of a second violation, both of which were committed within a period of twenty-four months, such person shall be punished by a fine of not less than two hundred dollars nor more than four hundred dollars; upon a conviction of a third or subsequent violation, all of which were committed within a period of twenty-four months, such person shall be punished by a fine of not less than four hundred dollars nor more than eight hundred dollars.

Part 3-A Penalties

§ 73-b. Misdemeanors

Every person convicted of a misdemeanor pursuant to any of the provisions of this chapter for which another penalty is not provided shall for a first conviction thereof be punished by a fine of not less than two hundred fifty nor more than five hundred dollars or by a period of imprisonment of not more than thirty days or by both such fine and imprisonment; for a conviction of a second violation, both of which were committed within a period of twenty-four months, such person shall be punished by a fine of not less than five hundred nor more than one thousand five hundred dollars or by a period of imprisonment of not more than sixty days or by both such fine and imprisonment; upon a conviction of a third or subsequent violation, all of which were committed within a period of twenty-four months, such person shall be punished by a fine of not less than one thousand five hundred nor more than two thousand five hundred dollars or by a period of imprisonment of not more than one hundred twenty days or by both such fine and imprisonment.

§ 73-c. Violations

1. Any person who violates any of the provisions of this article or any local law, ordinance, order, rule or regulation adopted pursuant to this article, shall be guilty of a violation unless such conduct is declared to be a misdemeanor or a felony pursuant to this chapter or any other law of this state.

2. Every person convicted of a violation for a violation of any of the provisions of this article or of any ordinance, order, rule or regulation adopted pursuant to this article for which another penalty is not provided shall for a first conviction thereof be punished by a fine of not less than one hundred nor more than two hundred fifty dollars or by imprisonment for

not more than seven days or by both such fine and imprisonment; for a conviction of a second violation, both of which were committed within a period of twenty-four months, such person shall be punished by a fine of not less than two hundred fifty nor more than five hundred dollars or by imprisonment of not more than fifteen days or by both such fine and imprisonment; upon a conviction for a third or subsequent violation, all of which were committed within a period of twenty-four months, such person shall be punished by a fine of not less than five hundred nor more than one thousand dollars or by imprisonment for not more than thirty days or by both such fine and imprisonment.

Part 4 Non-Resident Owners and Operators

§ 74. Service of summons and complaint on non-residents

1. The use, operation, navigation or maintenance by a non-resident, or in his business, of a vessel in waters of this state; or owned by a non-resident and used, operated, navigated or maintained with his permission in waters of this state, shall be deemed equivalent to an appointment by such non-resident of the secretary of state to be his true and lawful attorney upon whom may be served the summons and complaint in any action against him, growing out of any accident or collision in which such non-resident may be involved while using, operating, navigating or maintaining such vessel in waters of this state, or in which such vessel may be involved while being used, operated, navigated or maintained in such waters in the business of the non-resident, or with the permission, expressed [express]* or implied, of such non-resident, and such use, operation, navigation or maintenance shall be deemed a signification of his agreement that any such summons and complaint against him which is so served shall be of the same legal force and validity as if served upon him personally within the state and the territorial jurisdiction of the court from which the summons issues, and that such appointment of the secretary of state shall be irrevocable and binding upon his executor or administrator. Where such non-resident has died prior to the commencement of an action brought pursuant to this section, service of summons and complaint shall be made on the executor or administrator of such non-resident in the same manner and on the same notice as is provided in the case of the non-resident himself. Where an action has been duly commenced under the provisions of this section against a non-resident who dies thereafter, the court must allow the action to be continued against his executor or

administrator upon motion with such notice as the court deems proper.

2. A summons and complaint in an action described in this section may issue in any court in the state having jurisdiction of the subject matter and be served as hereinafter provided. Service of such summons and complaint shall be made by mailing a copy thereof to the secretary of state at his office in the city of Albany, or by personally delivering a copy thereof to one of his regularly established offices, with a fee of five dollars, and such service shall be sufficient service upon such non-resident provided that notice of such service and a copy of the summons and complaint are forthwith sent by or on behalf of the plaintiff to the defendant by registered mail with return receipt requested. The plaintiff shall file with the clerk of the court in which the action is pending, or with the judge or justice of such court in case there be no clerk, an affidavit of compliance herewith, a copy of the summons and complaint, and either a return receipt purporting to be signed by the defendant or a person qualified to receive his registered mail, in accordance with the rules and customs of the post office department; or, if acceptance was refused by the defendant or his agent, the original envelope bearing a notation by the postal authorities that receipt was refused, and an affidavit by or on behalf of the plaintiff that notice of such mailing and refusal was forthwith sent to the defendant by ordinary mail. Where the summons is mailed to a foreign country, other official proof of the delivery of the mail may be filed in case the post-office department is unable to obtain such a return receipt. The foregoing papers shall be filed within thirty days after the return receipt or other official proof of delivery or the original envelope bearing a notation of refusal, as the case may be, is received by the plaintiff. Service of process shall be complete when such papers are filed. The return receipt or other official proof of delivery shall constitute presumptive evidence that the summons mailed was received by the defendant or a person qualified to receive his registered mail; and the notation of refusal shall constitute presumptive evidence that the refusal was by the defendant or his agent. Service of such summons also may be made by mailing a copy thereof to the secretary of state at his office in the city of Albany, or by personally delivering a copy thereof to one of his regularly established offices, with a fee of five dollars, and by delivering a duplicate copy thereof, with the complaint annexed thereto, to the defendant personally without the state by a resident or citizen of the state of New York or a sheriff,

under-sheriff, deputy-sheriff or constable of the county or other political subdivision in which the personal service is made, or an officer authorized by the laws of this state, to take acknowledgments of deeds to be recorded in this state, or an attorney and/or counselor at law, solicitor, advocate or barrister duly qualified to practice in the state or country where such service is made, or by a United States marshal or deputy United States marshal. Proof of personal service without the state shall be filed with the clerk of the court in which the action is pending within thirty days after such service. Personal service without the state is complete when proof thereof is filed. The court in which the action is pending may order such extension as may be necessary to afford the defendant reasonable opportunity to defend the action.

3. Service of summons on residents who depart from state and on residents' executors or administrators who are nonresidents or who depart from state. The provisions of section seventy-four of this chapter shall also apply (a) to a resident who departs from the state subsequent to the accident or collision and remains absent therefrom for thirty days continuously, whether such absence is intended to be temporary or permanent, and to any executor or administrator of such resident, and (b) to an executor or administrator of a resident if such executor or administrator is a nonresident or if, being a resident, he departs from the state and remains absent therefrom for thirty days continuously, whether such absence is intended to be temporary or permanent.

4. As used in this section "vessel" means a vessel commonly known as a "houseboat" and every vessel or floating craft propelled in any manner, except a vessel having a valid marine document issued by the United States or a foreign government.

Part 5 Boating Safety Education

§ 75. Educational program

In order to protect the public interest in the prudent and equitable use of the waters of the state and enhance the enjoyment of pleasure boating and other sports thereon, the commissioner shall initiate and put into effect a comprehensive educational program designed to advance boating safety, which provides for the training of all boat operators in the safe operation of vessels including personal watercraft and specialty prop-craft.

§ 76. Information

Such program shall include the preparation and dissemination of water safety information to the public, and particularly to the owners and operators of pleasure boats.

§ 77. Rules and regulations

The commissioner may make rules and regulations designed to result in the further knowledge and observance of the principles of safe boat operation.

§ 78. Boating safety certificate

1. "Boating safety certificate" shall mean a certificate issued by the commissioner evidencing that the holder thereof has successfully completed a course of instruction in boating safety as provided in this section. The commissioner shall put into effect a plan for the training of all boat operators and the issuance of such boating safety certificates. For the purposes of this section, the term "boating safety" shall include instruction in the safe operation of personal watercraft and specialty prop-craft.

2. "Boating safety certificate" shall also mean a certificate issued by the commissioner evidencing that the holder thereof has successfully completed a course of instruction in the safe operation of vessels including personal watercraft and speciality prop-craft. The commissioner is authorized to collect a fee not to exceed ten dollars for the issuance of such certificate which fee shall be deposited in the "I love NY waterways" boating safety fund established by section ninety-seven-nn of the state finance law, as added by chapter eight hundred five of the laws of nineteen hundred ninety-two, and shall be solely available to support the administration of personal watercraft and specialty prop-craft safety training and enforcement.

3. The commissioner is authorized and directed to establish a system for tracking and replacing boating safety certificates issued by the commissioner. The commissioner is further authorized to require that any other entity approved by the commissioner to provide courses of instruction and award boating safety certificates establish a system for tracking and replacing boating safety certificates so as to enable the replacement of lost or stolen certificates to those who have previously been awarded such certificates.

§ 78-a. Insurance rate reduction

Any insurance carrier licensed to issue yacht or boating liability insurance in this state is authorized to grant rate reductions with the approval of the department of financial services to any owner of a yacht or boat who has successfully completed a boating safety course or holds a valid United States Coast Guard operators license.

§ 79. Courses of instruction

1. For the purpose of giving such courses of instruction and awarding boating safety certificates, the commissioner may designate as his or her agent any person the commissioner deems qualified to act in such capacity, including, but not limited to, certified instructors of the United States coast guard auxiliary, United States power squadrons, the United States sailing association for a powerboating course or courses which are approved by the commissioner, American power boat association, boy scouts of America, Red Cross and other organizations. No charge whatsoever shall be made to any person less than eighteen years of age for the issuance of a boating safety certificate. Persons less than eighteen years of age may be charged a fee for instruction in boating safety, except that the office may not charge a fee when providing such instruction to persons less than eighteen years of age.

2. The commissioner is authorized, at his or her discretion, to develop a method for approving internet-based boating safety courses as an appropriate and effective method for the administration and completion of training in the safe operation of vessels, including personal watercraft and specialty prop-craft, for the purposes of awarding a boating safety certificate pursuant to this section.

Article 4-A Enforcement by Counties

§ 79-a. Definitions

As used in this article:

1. "State aid" shall mean payments by the state to an eligible governmental entity in accordance with the provisions of this article.

2. "Program year" shall mean the calendar year.

2-a. "Eligible governmental entity" shall mean the Lake George park commission or a county enforcing the provisions of this chapter and having an accident reporting system and vessel and related equipment anti-theft program and/or an "I love NY waterways" boating safety program and/or boating noise level enforcement program approved by the commissioner. In a county which does not enforce the provisions of this chapter and has an approved accident reporting system and vessel and related equipment anti-theft program and/or an "I love NY waterways" boating safety program and/or a boating noise level enforcement program, the eligible governmental entity may be a city, town or village within the county. In addition, the commissioner shall promulgate regulations to provide for direct funding to any city, town or village in a county constituting an eligible governmental entity pursuant to this subdivision which such city, town or village enforces the provisions of this chapter and has established an "I love NY waterways" boating safety program approved by the commissioner.

3. "County, city, town or village" shall mean each county, city, town or village in the state of New York except those counties which lie within the territorial limits of the city of New York. The term "county" with reference to such counties lying within the territorial limits of the city of New York shall mean the city of New York.

4. "Authorized expenditures" shall mean those expenditures determined by the commissioner to be reasonable and necessary for the adequate and proper enforcement of the provisions of this chapter, and for implementing an accident reporting system and vessel and related equipment anti-theft program and/or an "I love NY waterways" boating safety program and/or a boating noise level enforcement program. The commissioner shall prepare and maintain in his office a schedule of such authorized expenditures and amend the same from time to time.

§ 79-b. Vessel and equipment anti-theft program; eligibility for state aid

1. The commissioner of parks, recreation and historic preservation shall establish a vessel and related equipment anti-theft program, which shall be applicable on all waterways or bodies of water located within New York state or that part of any body of water adjacent to New York state over which the state has territorial jurisdiction, and on which watercraft may be used or operated. Such program shall include, but need not be limited to provisions relating to the reporting of vessel and related equipment theft, the dissemination of information relating to vessel and related equipment theft, personnel training, the

establishment of a system to aid in the identification of stolen vessels and related law enforcement functions.

1-a. [There are two subs 1-a] The commissioner shall establish an "I love NY waterways" boating safety program which shall be applicable on the navigable waters of the state or any tidewaters bordering on or lying within the boundaries of Nassau and Suffolk counties. Such program shall include boating safety and accident prevention education and measures to reduce alcohol-related boating accidents and injuries.

1-a. [There are two subs 1-a] The commissioner shall establish a boating noise level enforcement program which shall be applicable on the navigable waters of the state or any tidewaters bordering on or lying within the boundaries of Nassau and Suffolk counties.

2. Each eligible governmental entity shall be entitled to receive state aid as hereinafter provided. An entity seeking reimbursement for expenditures incurred in enforcement of this chapter and participation in approved accident reporting and anti-theft programs and/or an "I love NY waterways" boating safety program and/or a boating noise level enforcement program shall submit to the commissioner by October first of each year an estimate of such expenditures for the current calendar year, in such form and containing such information as he may require. Within one month after the close of the calendar year, it shall submit to the commissioner a statement of authorized expenditures actually incurred, in such form and containing such information as he may require.

3. The amount of state aid to be allocated to eligible governmental entities pursuant to this article shall be determined by the commissioner as hereinafter provided. The commissioner shall determine the percentage proportion which the authorized expenditures of each individual entity, not exceeding four hundred thousand dollars for each county including municipalities therein, shall bear to the total authorized expenditures of all entities. Such percentage proportion shall then be applied against an amount equal to one-half of the total of the amount received by the state in each preceding program year in vessel registration fees as provided in section twenty-two hundred fifty-one of the vehicle and traffic law, less no more than thirty percent, subject to appropriation, which may be used by the commissioner and the commissioner of motor vehicles for administrative costs of the program, including training and equipment, and by the department of environmental

conservation, the division of state police and other state agencies, subject to the approval of the commissioner, for the purposes of this article, plus the entire amount received pursuant to subdivision nine of section forty-four of this chapter. The amount thus determined shall constitute the maximum amount of state aid to which each such entity shall be entitled; provided, however, that no entity shall receive state aid in an amount in excess of fifty percent of its authorized expenditures as approved by the commissioner for such program year. The commissioner shall certify to the comptroller the amount thus determined for each eligible local governmental entity as the amount of state aid to be apportioned to such eligible local governmental entity. The allocation of state aid to any county, town or village within the Lake George park shall not be reduced because of the allocation of state aid to the Lake George park commission. Of the remaining funds received by the state for the registration of vessels as provided in section twenty-two hundred fifty-one of the vehicle and traffic law, no less than six percent shall be made available to the commissioner for the expenses of the office in providing navigation law enforcement training and administering the provisions of this section.

4. The amount of funds historically appropriated by any municipality receiving funding pursuant to this article shall not be reduced because of the availability of appropriations from such fund.

§ 79-c. Rules

The commissioner may adopt and amend when he deems necessary all rules and regulations to carry out the provisions of this article.

Article 12 Oil Spill Prevention, Control, and Compensation

Part ONE General Provisions

§ 170. Legislative intent

The legislature finds and declares that New York's lands and waters constitute a unique and delicately balanced resource; that the protection and preservation of these lands and waters promotes the health, safety and welfare of the people of this state; that the tourists and recreation industry dependent on clean waters and beaches is vital to the economy of this state; that the state is the trustee, for the benefit of its citizens, of all natural resources within its jurisdiction; and that the storage and transfer of petroleum between vessels, between facilities and vessels, and between facilities, whether onshore or offshore, is a hazardous undertaking and imposes risks of damage to persons and property within this state.

The legislature finds and declares that the discharge of petroleum within or outside the jurisdiction of this state constitutes a threat to the economy and environment of this state. The legislature intends by the passage of this article to exercise the powers of this state to control the transfer and storage of petroleum and to provide liability for damage sustained within this state as a result of the discharge of said petroleum by requiring prompt cleanup and removal of such pollution and petroleum, and to provide a fund for swift and adequate compensation to resort businesses and other persons damaged by such discharge.

§ 171. Purposes

It is the purpose of this article to ensure a clean environment and healthy economy for the state by preventing the unregulated discharge of petroleum which may result in damage to lands, waters or natural resources of the state by authorizing the department of environmental conservation to respond quickly to such discharges and effect prompt cleanup and removal of such discharges, giving first priority to minimizing environmental damage, and by providing for liability for damage sustained within the state as a result of such discharges.

§ 172. Definitions

Unless the context clearly indicates otherwise, the following terms shall have the following meanings:

1. "Administrator" means the chief executive, within the department of audit and control, of the New York environmental protection and spill compensation fund;

2. "Barrel" means forty-two United States gallons, or 159.9 liters, at sixty degrees fahrenheit;

2-a. "Biological additives" means microbiological cultures, enzymes, or nutrient additives that are deliberately introduced into a petroleum discharge for the specific purpose of encouraging biodegradation to mitigate the effects of the discharge.

3. "Claim" means, for purposes of part three of this article, any claim of the fund or any claim by an injured person, who is not responsible for the discharge, seeking compensation for cleanup and removal costs incurred or damages sustained as a result of a petroleum discharge;

3-a. "Burning agents" means additives that, through physical or chemical means, improve the combustibility of the materials to which they are applied.

3-b. "Chemical agents" means generally those elements, compounds or mixtures that coagulate, disperse, dissolve, emulsify, foam, neutralize, precipitate, reduce, solubilize, oxidize, concentrate, congeal, entrap, fix, make the pollutant mass more rigid or viscous, or otherwise facilitate the mitigation of deleterious effects or removal of the pollutant or petroleum from the water.

4. "Cleanup and removal" means the (a) containment or attempted containment of a discharge, (b) removal or attempted removal of a discharge or, (c) taking of reasonable measures to prevent or mitigate damages to the public health, safety, or welfare, including but not limited to, public and private property, shorelines, beaches, surface waters, water columns and bottom sediments, soils and other affected property, including wildlife and other natural resources;

5. "Cleanup and removal costs" means all costs associated with the cleanup and removal of a discharge including relocation costs pursuant to section one hundred seventy-seven-a of this article incurred by the state or its political subdivisions or their agents or any person with approval of the department;

6. "Commissioner" means the commissioner of the department of environmental conservation, unless otherwise indicated;

6-a. "Containment boom" means a floating or stationary device composed of plastic, natural or synthetic materials which can be mechanically extended over water or permanently stationed over water for the purposes of containing floating petroleum, solid objects or other pollutants within or outside a particular area;

7. "Department" means the department of environmental conservation, unless otherwise indicated;

8. "Discharge" means any intentional or unintentional action or omission resulting in

the releasing, spilling, leaking, pumping, pouring, emitting, emptying or dumping of petroleum into the waters of the state or onto lands from which it might flow or drain into said waters, or into waters outside the jurisdiction of the state when damage may result to the lands, waters or natural resources within the jurisdiction of the state;

8-a. "Dispersant" means chemical agents that emulsify, disperse, or solubilize petroleum into the water column or promote the surface spreading of petroleum slicks to facilitate dispersal of the petroleum into the water column.

9. "Fund" means the New York environmental protection and spill compensation fund;

10. "License fee period" means every calendar month on the basis of which the licensee is required to report under this article;

11. "Major facility" includes but is not limited to any refinery, storage or transfer terminal, pipeline, deep water port, drilling platform or any appurtenance related to any of the preceding that is used or is capable of being used to refine, produce, store, handle, transfer, process or transport petroleum. A vessel shall be considered a major facility only when petroleum is transferred between vessels. A vessel that would not otherwise be considered a major facility shall not be considered a major facility based solely upon its rendering of care, assistance or advice consistent with the national contingency plan or as otherwise directed by the federal on-scene coordinator or by the commissioner or his designee, in response to a discharge of petroleum into or upon the navigable waters. Facilities with total combined above-ground or buried storage capacity of less than four hundred thousand gallons are not major facilities for the purposes of this article;

12. "Natural resources" means all land, fish, shellfish, wildlife, biota, air, waters and other such resources;

13. "Owner" or "operator" means with respect to a vessel, any person owning, operating or chartering by demise such vessel; with respect to any major facility, any person owning such facility, or operating it by lease, contract or other form of agreement; with respect to abandoned or derelict major facilities, the person who owned or operated such facility immediately prior to such abandonment, or the owner at the time of discharge;

14. "Person" means public or private corporations, companies, associations, societies, firms, partnerships, joint stock companies, individuals, the United States, the state of New

York and any of its political subdivisions or agents;

15. "Petroleum" means oil or petroleum of any kind and in any form including, but not limited to, oil, petroleum, fuel oil, oil sludge, oil refuse, oil mixed with other wastes and crude oils, gasoline and kerosene;

15-a. "Petroleum-bearing vessel" means any vessel transporting petroleum in commercial quantities as cargo or any vessel constructed or adapted for the carriage of petroleum in bulk;

15-b. "Sinking agents" means additives applied to petroleum discharges to sink floating pollutants below the water surface.

15-c. "Surface collecting agents" means chemical agents that form a surface film to control the layer thickness of petroleum.

15-d. "Tank vessel" means a vessel that is constructed or adapted to carry, or that carries, petroleum in bulk as cargo or cargo residue, and that:

(a) is a vessel of the United States;

(b) operates on the waters of the state of New York; or

(c) transfers petroleum in a place subject to the jurisdiction of the [of the]* state of New York.

16. "Transfer" means onloading or offloading between major facilities and vessels or vessels and major facilities, and from vessel to vessel or major facility to major facility;

17. "Vessel" means every description, of watercraft or other contrivance that is practically capable of being used as a means of commercial transportation of petroleum upon the water, whether or not self-propelled; and

18. "Waters" means the ocean and its estuaries to the seaward limit of the state's jurisdiction, and all lakes, springs, streams and bodies of surface or groundwater, whether natural or artificial, within the boundaries of this state. Provided, however, that for purposes of this definition, waters of the state adjacent to Long Island Sound are to be strictly construed to effectuate only the provisions of this article.

Part TWO Oil Spill Cleanup and Removal; Licenses

§ 173. Discharge of petroleum; prohibition

1. The discharge of petroleum is prohibited.

2. On or after January first, nineteen hundred ninety-four, all new vessels sold in New York that are equipped with fuel tank air vents shall have such fuel tank air vents designed to prevent fuel overflow during refueling. The provisions of this subdivision shall not apply to those fuel systems in vessels which are required to meet the standards provided for in the Federal Boat Safety Act of 1971.

3. This section shall not apply to discharges of petroleum pursuant to and in compliance with the conditions of a federal or state permit.

§ 174. Licenses

1. No person shall operate or cause to be operated a major facility as defined in this article without (a) a license issued by the commissioner, (b) without paying a license fee if such fee is required by the administrator, pursuant to the provisions of paragraph (a) of subdivision four of this section, and (c) without paying the surcharge established by paragraph (b) of subdivision four of this section.

2. Licenses shall be issued for a period not to exceed five years, subject to such terms and conditions as the department may determine are necessary to carry out the purposes of this article.

3. As a condition precedent to the issuance or renewal of a license the department shall require satisfactory evidence that the applicant has implemented or is in the process of implementing state and federal plans and regulations for control of discharges of petroleum, and the containment and removal thereof when a discharge occurs.

4.

(a) The license fee shall be nine and one-half cents per barrel transferred, provided, however, that the fee on any barrel, including any products derived therefrom, subject to multiple transfer, shall be imposed only once at the point of first transfer. Provided further, the license fee for major facilities that (i) transfer barrels for their own use, and (ii) do not sell or transfer the product subject to such license fee, shall be eight cents. In each fiscal year following any year in which the balance of the account established by paragraph (a) of subdivision two of section one hundred seventy-nine of this article equals or exceeds forty million dollars, no license fee shall be imposed unless (a) the current balance in such account is less than thirty-five million dollars or (b) pending claims against such account exceed fifty percent of the existing balance of such account. In the event of either such occurrence and upon certification thereof by the state comptroller, the administrator shall within ten days of the date of such certification reimpose the license fee, which shall take effect on the first day of the month following such relevy. The rate may be set at less than nine and one-half cents per barrel transferred if the administrator determines that the revenue produced by such lower rate shall be sufficient to pay outstanding claims against such account within one year of such imposition of the license fee. Should such account exceed forty million dollars, as a result of interest, the administrator and the commissioner of environmental conservation shall report to the legislature and the governor concerning the options for the use of such interest. The fee established by this paragraph shall not be imposed upon any barrel which is transferred to a land based facility but thereafter exported from this state for use outside the state and is shipped to facilities outside the state regardless of whether the delivery or sale of such petroleum occurs in this state.

(b) The surcharge on the license fee shall be four and one-quarter cents per barrel for each barrel transferred on or after February first, nineteen hundred ninety.

(c) The surcharge established by paragraph (b) of this subdivision shall continue to be paid despite the fact that the license fee imposed pursuant to paragraph (a) of this subdivision may, pursuant to said paragraph, no longer be imposed.

(d) The surcharge established by paragraph (b) of this subdivision shall be thirteen and three quarters cents per barrel for any barrel that is transferred but thereafter exported from this state for use outside the state as described by paragraph (a) of this subdivision. Twelve and one-quarter cents of such surcharge shall be credited to the account established by paragraph (a) of subdivision two of section one hundred seventy-nine of this article.

5. Every licensee required to pay a major petroleum license fee or surcharge pursuant to paragraph (a) or (b) of subdivision four of this section shall on or before the twentieth day of the month following the close of each license fee period certify to the commissioner on such forms as may be prescribed by the commissioner the number of barrels of petroleum transferred to the licensee's major facility during the license fee period and at the same time shall pay the full amount of the license fee and surcharge due except that no licensee shall be required to make such payment until the cumulative amount due equals or exceeds

one hundred dollars. Any licensee whose cumulative license fee or surcharge does not equal or exceed one hundred dollars annually shall pay the total amount due on or before the twentieth day following the expiration date of the license issued pursuant to this section. Licensees who did not have to pay the license fee or surcharge shall certify annually to the commissioner on a form as may be prescribed by the commissioner on or before the twentieth day of April that the barrels of petroleum transferred to the licensee's major facility were not subject to the license fee or surcharge.

6. If a certificate required by this section is not filed, or if a certificate when filed is incorrect or insufficient in the opinion of the commissioner, the amount of license fee or surcharge due shall be determined by the commissioner from such information as may be available. Notice of such determination, and notice of licensee's right to appeal such determination, shall be given to the licensee liable for the payment of the license fee or surcharge. Such determination shall finally and irrevocably fix the fee or surcharge unless the person against whom it is assessed, within thirty days after receiving notice of such determination, shall apply to the commissioner for a hearing, or unless the commissioner on his own motion shall redetermine the same. After such hearing the commissioner shall give notice of his determination to the person to whom the license fee or surcharge is assessed.

7. Any licensee failing to file a certificate, failing to pay a license fee or surcharge, or filing or causing to be filed, a certificate which is willfully false, or failing to keep any records required by this article or rules and regulations adopted hereunder, shall, in addition to any other penalties herein or otherwise provided, be subject to a fine not to exceed two times the annual license fee or surcharge, as determined by the commissioner.

8. Within three months of the effective date of this article every owner or operator of a major facility shall obtain a license. The department shall issue a license upon the showing that such registrant can provide necessary equipment to prevent, contain and remove discharges of petroleum.

9. On or after June twenty-ninth, nineteen hundred seventy-eight, no person shall operate or cause to be operated any major facility without a major facility license issued by the commissioner. No license shall be valid for more than five years. Each applicant for a major facility license shall submit information, in a form satisfactory to the commissioner,

describing the following:

(a) The number of barrels or another measurement of the storage capacity of the facility;

(b) Average daily throughput of the facility;

(c) A primary and contingency cleanup and removal plan which includes, but is not limited to, an inventory of:

(i) The storage and transfer capacity of the facility;

(ii) The containment and removal equipment, including, but not limited to, vehicles, vessels, pumps, skimmers, booms, chemicals, and communication devices, to which the facility has access through direct ownership or by contract or membership in a discharge cleanup organization recognized by the departments of environmental conservation and transportation as well as the time lapse following a discharge which precedes such access;

(iii) The trained personnel which are required and available to operate such containment and removal equipment and the time lapse following a discharge which precedes such availability;

(iv) All equipment and trained personnel used or employed in a capacity at the facility to prevent discharges of petroleum;

(v) The terms of agreement and operation plan of any discharge cleanup organization to which the owner or operator of the facility belongs;

(vi) The type and amount of petroleum transferred, refined, processed or stored at the facility;

(d) The steps taken to insure prevention of a discharge;

10. No portion of fees or surcharges assessed and collected pursuant to this section shall be used for any purpose if such use, under federal law, would preclude the collection of such fee or surcharge.

11. Each owner or operator of a major facility or vessel subject to the provisions of this article shall designate a person in the state as his legal agent for service of process under this section and such designation shall be filed with the secretary of state. In the absence of such designation the secretary of state shall be the designated agent for purposes of service of process under this section.

§ 174-a. Use of containment booms.

1. The commissioner, after consultation with appropriate federal, state and local governments and agencies, may promulgate regulations requiring the use of containment booms or prestaging of response equipment around or at major facilities and vessels involved in the transfer of petroleum. The commissioner may consult with interested groups and trade associations in developing such regulations. In adopting such regulations, the commissioner shall consider factors, including but not limited to applicable federal laws and regulations, weather conditions, tides, health and safety of workers and product being transferred.

2. Whenever petroleum is transferred after sunset and before sunrise, lighting adequate to detect any petroleum discharge shall be in operation.

3. The deployment of containment booms pursuant to this part shall be the responsibility of the owner, lessee or operator of the vessels involved in a vessel-to-vessel petroleum transfer. The deployment of containment booms pursuant to this part shall be the responsibility of the owner, lessee or operator of the major facility involved in a petroleum transfer between a vessel and a major facility.

4.

(a) Any local law or ordinance which is inconsistent with any provision of this part or any rule or regulation promulgated hereunder shall be preempted, except that any local law or ordinance of any county, or of any city of a population of one million or more, which is inconsistent with the provisions of this part or any rules or regulations promulgated hereunder shall not be preempted if such local law or ordinance provides environmental protection equal to or greater than the provisions of this part of any rules or regulations promulgated hereunder, and such county or city files with the department a written declaration of its intent to administer and enforce such local law or ordinance which is approved by the commissioner in written findings which set forth the terms of such approval.

(b) Any owner, lessee or operator violating any provisions of this section or any rule promulgated thereunder shall: (i) if the transfer involves and/or the vessel contains less than one million gallons, be liable for a penalty of not more than twenty-five thousand dollars for each offense in a court of competent jurisdiction; or (ii) if the transfer involves and/or the vessel contains one million gallons or more, be liable for a penalty of not more than fifty thousand dollars for each offense in a court of competent jurisdiction. Every violation of this section shall be a separate and distinct offense, and, in case of a continuing violation, every day's continuance thereof shall be deemed to be a separate and distinct offense.

(c) All penalties and fines imposed under this section shall be credited to the New York environmental protection and spill compensation fund pursuant to paragraph (a) of subdivision two of section one hundred seventy-nine of this chapter.

§ 174-b. Use of agents

1. The commissioner may promulgate regulations governing the use of dispersants, burning agents, biological additives, surface collecting agents or other chemical additives in the cleanup and removal of a petroleum discharge.

2. The commissioner shall pursue an official memorandum of understanding with the United States Coast Guard regarding the planned uses of dispersants, burning agents, sinking agents, biological additives, surface collecting agents or other chemical additives in the event of a petroleum discharge. Such memorandum of understanding should be reflective of any rules or regulations promulgated pursuant to this section.

3. No person shall supervise, aid or participate in any use of dispersants, burning agents, sinking agents, biological additives, surface collecting agents or other chemical additives which is inconsistent with any rule or regulation promulgated pursuant to this section.

§ 175. Notification by persons responsible for discharge

Any person responsible for causing a discharge shall immediately notify the department pursuant to rules and regulations established by the department, but in no case later than two hours after the discharge. Failure to so notify shall make persons liable to the penalty provisions of section 192 of this article. Notwithstanding the provisions of any other law, such notification to the department shall be deemed to fulfill the notification requirements of any other state or local law.

§ 176. Removal of prohibited discharges

1. Any person discharging petroleum in the manner prohibited by section one hundred seventy-three of this article shall immediately undertake to contain such discharge. Notwithstanding the above requirement, the department may undertake the removal of

such discharge and may retain agents and contractors who shall operate under the direction of such department for such purposes. The commissioner shall develop a system of immediate response type contracts with appropriate agents and contractors. Such contracts shall be subject to the approval of the state comptroller in accordance with section one hundred twelve of the state finance law, however, such approval shall not obligate to any particular contract any specific amount of monies from the fund but shall obligate from the fund on an individual basis as such contracts are utilized the actual amount required to effectuate any contract or any portion thereof. Any necessary approvals of availability of funds for a particular project in accordance with any provision of the state finance law shall be undertaken as soon as practical after clean up and removal procedures are undertaken, or such procedures are ordered by the commissioner.

2.

(a) Upon the occurrence of a discharge of petroleum, the department shall respond promptly and proceed to cleanup and remove the discharge in accordance with environmental priorities or may, at its discretion, direct the discharger to promptly cleanup and remove the discharge. The department shall be responsible for cleanup and removal or as the case may be, for retaining agents and contractors who shall operate under the direction of that department for such purposes. Implementation of cleanup and removal procedures after each discharge shall be conducted in accordance with environmental priorities and procedures established by the department.

(b) Section eight of the court of claims act or any other provision of law to the contrary notwithstanding, the state shall be immune from liability and action with respect to any act or omission done in the discharge of the department's responsibility pursuant to this article; provided, however, that this subdivision shall not limit any liability which may otherwise exist for unlawful, willful or malicious acts or omissions on the part of the state, state agencies, or their officers, employees or agents or for a discharge in violation of section one hundred seventy-three of this article.

3. Any unexplained discharge of petroleum within state jurisdiction or discharge of petroleum occurring in waters beyond state jurisdiction that for any reason penetrates within state jurisdiction shall be removed by or under the direction of the department. Except for

those expenses incurred by the party causing such discharge, any expenses incurred in the removal of discharges shall be paid promptly from the New York environmental protection and spill compensation fund pursuant to sections one hundred and eighty-six and one hundred seventy-nine-a of this article and any reimbursements due such fund shall be collected in accordance with the provisions of section one hundred and eighty-seven of this article.

4. Cleanup and removal of petroleum and actions to minimize damage from discharges shall be, to the greatest extent possible, in accordance with the National Contingency Plan for removal of oil and hazardous substances established pursuant to section 311(d) of the Federal Water Pollution Control Act (33 U.S.C. 1251 et seq.), as amended by the Federal Oil Pollution Act of 1990 (33 U.S.C. 2701 et seq.), or revised under section 105 of the Comprehensive Environmental Response, Compensation, and Liability Act (42 U.S.C. 9605).

5. The department in consultation with the attorney general shall develop a standard contract form to be used when contracting services for the cleanup and removal of a discharge.

6. Whenever the department acts to remove a discharge or contracts to secure prospective removal services, it is authorized to draw upon the money available in the fund. Such moneys shall be used to pay promptly for all cleanup and removal costs incurred by the department.

7.

(a) Nothing in this section is intended to preclude cleanup and removal by any person threatened by such discharges, who, as soon as is reasonably possible, coordinates and obtains approval for such actions with ongoing state or federal operations and appropriate state and federal authorities. Notwithstanding any other provision of law to the contrary, the liability of any contractor for such person, where such person obtains approval from appropriate state and federal authorities for such cleanup and removal, and the liability of any person providing services related to the cleanup or removal of a discharge, under contract with the department, for any injury to a person or property caused by or related to such services shall be limited to acts or omissions of the person during the course of performing such services which are shown to have been the result of negligence, gross negligence or reckless, wanton or intentional misconduct. Notwithstanding any other provisions of law, when (i) a verdict or decision in an action or claim for injury to a person or property caused by or related to such services is determined in favor of a claimant in an action involving a person performing such services and any other person or persons jointly liable, and (ii) the liability of the person performing such services is found to be fifty percent or less of the total liability assigned to all persons liable, and (iii) the liability of the person performing such services is not based on a finding of reckless disregard for the safety of others, or intentional misconduct, then the liability of the person performing such services to the claimant for loss relating to injury to property and for non-economic loss relating to injury to a person shall not exceed the equitable share of the person performing such services determined in accordance with the relative culpability of each person causing or contributing to the total liability for such losses; provided, however, that the culpable conduct of any person not a party to the action shall not be considered in determining any equitable share herein if the claimant proves that with due diligence the claimant was unable to obtain jurisdiction over such person in said action. As used in this section, the term "non-economic loss" includes, but is not limited to, pain and suffering, mental anguish, loss of consortium or other damages for non-economic loss. However, nothing in this subdivision shall be deemed to alter, modify or abrogate the liability of any person performing such services for breach of any express warranty, limited or otherwise, or an express or implied warranty under the uniform commercial code, or to an employee of such person pursuant to the workers' compensation law, or to relieve from any liability any person who is responsible for a discharge in violation of section one hundred seventy-four of this article.

(b)   No action taken by any person to contain or remove a discharge shall be construed as an admission of liability for said discharge. No person who gratuitously renders assistance in containing or removing a discharge shall be liable for any civil damages to third parties resulting solely from acts or omissions of such person in rendering such assistance except for acts or omissions of gross negligence or willful misconduct. In the course of cleanup and removal, no person shall discharge any detergent into the waters of this state without prior authorization of the commissioner of environmental conservation.

(c)   A person may, without admission of responsibility for the discharge of petroleum and with the consent of the commissioner, commence clean up and removal of the discharge and upon the recommendation of the commissioner of health and with the consent of the fund undertake the relocation of persons affected by the discharge of petroleum. Upon determination by the fund that the person is not responsible for the discharge, the person shall be reimbursed by the fund for the actual and necessary expenses incurred.

8. Notwithstanding any other provision of law to the contrary, including but not limited to section 15-108 of the general obligations law, every person providing cleanup, removal of discharge of petroleum or relocation of persons pursuant to this section shall be entitled to contribution from any other responsible party.

§ 177. Emergency oil spill control network

1. The commissioner shall establish an emergency oil spill control network which shall be comprised of available equipment from appropriate town, county and state highway departments. Such network shall be employed to provide an immediate response to a discharge on any of the waters of the state. Furthermore, such network shall be employed in conjunction with the cleanup operations of the owner or operator, the department and any federal agency.

2. The commissioner shall make an inventory of all equipment in town, county, and state highway departments that would be capable of participating in discharge cleanup operations.

3. The commissioner shall have the power to deploy such equipment to participate in a discharge cleanup operation at his discretion and to reimburse such town, county, and state highway departments for use of such equipment from the fund.

4. The commissioner may request and shall receive from any other state agency such assistance and data as will enable him to carry out his responsibilities pursuant to this section.

5.

(a) The commissioner shall issue a catalogue designed to expedite responses to discharges of petroleum.

(b) The catalogue shall contain the following information, broken down by geographical area:

(i) a listing of state stand-by contractors, their equipment and spill response capabilities;

(ii) a listing of state-owned equipment which could be used in the event of a major discharge of petroleum;

(iii) a listing of companies and organizations that have spill response equipment available for sale, lease or loan; and

(iv) a listing of organizations which are involved in the cleanup and rehabilitation of birds and wildlife.

(c) The catalogue shall be updated as deemed appropriate by the commissioner.

(d) The commissioner shall notify the chief executive officer of all counties which border on any navigable waters of the state or on the marine and coastal district, as defined in section 13-0303 of the environmental conservation law, of the availability of the catalogue. This catalogue shall be distributed upon request at a maximum fee of twenty-five cents per page. Any such fee shall be deposited into the New York environmental protection and spill compensation fund established pursuant to section one hundred seventy-nine of this article.

6. The commissioner may institute a program to educate local officials on procedures to follow in reporting and responding to spill emergencies.

§ 177-a. Emergency oil spill relocation network

1. The commissioner shall establish an emergency oil spill relocation network which shall be headed by the commissioner of health and comprised of the appropriate services from county and state health departments.

2. Such network shall be employed to provide an immediate response to a discharge in any area of the state where the public health may be at risk. Further, such network shall be employed in conjunction with the cleanup operations of the owner or operator, the department or any federal agency.

3. The commissioner of health shall be first notified whenever an application is made for emergency oil spill relocation.

4. The commissioner of health shall have the power to deploy such resources at his discretion to the state and local health departments to make an assessment of the possible health risks to persons residing in the area of the spill site.

5. The commissioner of health shall determine the actual and necessary costs of the relocation of individuals who, in his opinion, are exposed to health risks as a result of the discharge and certify the amount of such costs to the administrator. The certification by the

commissioner of health shall be for a period of relocation not exceeding thirty days, provided that the commissioner upon a further assessment of the possible health risks in the area of the spill site may extend such relocation for successive thirty day periods. The certification by the commissioner of health shall not be admissible in any civil action in a court of law in regard to the issue of damages to the individuals certified for relocation pursuant to this section.

6. Notwithstanding any provision of law to the contrary the certification of individuals for relocation and its associated costs shall be an issue restricted to consideration as cleanup cost and shall not be a determination of liability, nor shall it be admissible in any civil action in a court of law in regard to the issue of damages to the individuals certified for relocation pursuant to this section.

7. The commissioner of health may request and shall receive from the department and any other state agency such assistance and data as will enable him to carry out his responsibilities pursuant to this section.

§ 177-b. Habitat protection plan

The commissioner may require every major facility which engages in the transfer of petroleum to file with the department a habitat protection plan as a condition of issuance of a license pursuant to section one hundred seventy-four of this article. Such plan shall provide protection from the potential adverse impact of any discharge on the habitat of threatened or endangered species and the mitigation of potential damage to wetlands in reasonable proximity to the facility. Such plan shall contain provisions for the rehabilitation of animals damaged by the discharge of petroleum.

§ 178. Right to enter and inspect

The department is hereby authorized to enter and inspect any property or premises for the purpose of inspecting facilities and investigating either actual or suspected sources of discharges or violation of this article or any rule or regulation promulgated pursuant to this article. The department is further authorized to enter on property or premises in order to assist in the cleanup or removal of the discharge. Any information relating to secret processes or methods of manufacture shall be kept confidential.

§ 178-a. Responder immunity

1. Definitions. For the purposes of this section only, the following terms shall have the following meanings:

(a) "response efforts" means rendering care, assistance, or advice in accordance with the national contingency plan, the state oil spill contingency plan, or at the direction of the federal on-scene coordinator or the commissioner or his designee, in response to a discharge or threatened discharge of petroleum into or upon the navigable waters.

(b) "responsible party" and "navigable waters" shall have the meanings set forth in section 1001 of the Federal Oil Pollution Act of 1990 (33 U.S.C. 2701 et seq.).

2. Notwithstanding any other provision of law,

(a) a person is not liable for cleanup and removal costs or damages which result from actions taken or omitted to be taken in good faith in the course of rendering care, assistance or advice consistent with the national contingency plan or as otherwise directed by the federal on-scene coordinator or by the commissioner or his designee, in response to a discharge or threatened discharge of petroleum into or upon the navigable waters.

(b) A person holding a master's or a towing vessel operator's license, the owner, and operator of a vessel operated by such person are not liable for cleanup and removal costs or damages which result from actions taken in good faith in the course of rendering assistance, in an emergency situation, at the request of the owner or operator of a vessel attempting to prevent the substantial threat of a discharge of petroleum into or upon the navigable waters; provided, however, that reasonable efforts are made to notify the federal on-scene coordinator or the commissioner or his designee prior to such assistance being rendered or, if that is not practicable, as soon as possible thereafter.

3. However, the provisions of subdivision two of this section shall not apply to: (i) a responsible party, (ii) liability for personal injury or wrongful death, (iii) cleanup and removal costs and damages resulting from such person's gross negligence or willful misconduct, (iv) negligence in the operation of a motor vehicle as defined in section one hundred twenty-five of the vehicle and traffic law, and (v) any physical actions taken that are not in or near the area of cleanup and removal of a discharge or threatened discharge.

4. The provisions of subdivision two of this section shall not apply to any response efforts

undertaken by a person later than one hundred twenty days after a discharge has been stopped. Thereafter, such person shall not be strictly liable without regard to fault, but the liability of such person for personal injury or property damage shall be limited to acts or omissions of the person during the course of such response efforts which are shown to be the result of negligence, gross negligence, or reckless, wanton or intentional misconduct. Notwithstanding any other provision of law, when (i) a verdict or decision on a claim for injury to persons or property caused by response efforts, occurring after such one hundred twenty day period has ended, is determined in favor of the claimant in an action involving such person's response efforts and any other person or persons jointly liable, and (ii) the liability of the person related to such response efforts is found to be fifty percent or less of the total liability assigned to all persons liable, and (iii) the liability of the person related to such response efforts is not based on a finding of reckless disregard for the safety of others or of intentional misconduct, then the liability of such person to the claimant for injury to property and for non-economic loss relating to injury to a person shall not exceed the equitable share of such person as determined in accordance with the relative culpability of each person causing or contributing to the total liability. Provided, however, the culpable conduct of any person not a party to such action shall not be considered in determining any equitable share if the claimant was unable, with due diligence, to obtain jurisdiction over such person in said action. As used in this section, "non-economic loss" includes but is not limited to pain and suffering, mental anguish, loss of consortium or other damages for non-economic loss. However, nothing herein shall alter, modify, or abrogate the liability of any person for breach of warranty or to an employee of such person pursuant to the workers' compensation law, or to relieve from liability any person who is responsible for a discharge in violation of section one hundred seventy-four of this article.

5. In addition to any other liability, a responsible party shall be liable for any cleanup and removal costs and damages that another person is relieved of under subdivision two or four or both of this section.

6. Nothing in this section affects (i) the obligation of a discharger to respond immediately and to cleanup and remove a discharge; or (ii) the liability of a discharger under other provisions of this article or the environmental conservation law.

Part THREE New York Environmental Protection and Spill Compensation Fund; Liability; Third Party Compensation

§ 179. New York environmental protection and spill compensation fund

1. The New York environmental protection and spill compensation fund is hereby established as a nonlapsing, revolving fund in the department of audit and control to carry out the purposes of this article.

2. Two separate accounts are hereby established within the fund established by subdivision one of this section:

(a) An account which shall be credited with all license fees and penalties collected pursuant to paragraph (b) of subdivision one and paragraph (a) of subdivision four of section one hundred seventy-four of this article except as provided in section one hundred seventy-nine-a of this article, the portion of the surcharge collected pursuant to paragraph (d) of subdivision four of section one hundred seventy-four of this article, penalties collected pursuant to paragraph (b) of subdivision four of section one hundred seventy-four-a of this article, money collected pursuant to section one hundred eighty-seven of this article, all penalties collected pursuant to section one hundred ninety-two of this article, and registration fees collected pursuant to subdivision two of section 17-1009 of the environmental conservation law.

(b) An account which shall be credited with all surcharges collected pursuant to paragraph (c) of subdivision one and paragraph (b) of subdivision four of section one hundred seventy-four of this article. In addition, such account shall be credited with funds from the account established by paragraph (a) of this subdivision in an amount equal to two and three-quarters cents multiplied by the number of barrels of petroleum subject to the provisions of paragraph (d) of subdivision four of section one hundred seventy-four of this article. The amount so credited shall not exceed the amount equal to two and three-quarters cents multiplied by the number of barrels which would have been subject to the provisions of such paragraph (d) during the state fiscal year ending March thirty-first, nineteen hundred ninety-nine.

Interest received on moneys in each account in the fund shall be credited to that account, respectively.

§ 179-a. New York environmental protection and spill remediation account

1. There is hereby created an account within the miscellaneous capital projects fund, the New York environmental protection and spill remediation account. The New York environmental protection and spill remediation account shall consist of license fees received by the state pursuant to section one hundred seventy-four of this article, in an amount equal to expenditures made from this account.

2. These moneys, after appropriation by the legislature, and within the amounts set forth and for the several purposes specified, shall be available to reimburse the department of environmental conservation for expenditures associated with the purposes of costs incurred under this article, including cleanup and removal of petroleum spills, and other capital, investigation, maintenance and remediation costs.

3. All payments made from the New York environmental protection and spill remediation account shall be made by the administrator upon certification by the commissioner.

4. Spending pursuant to this section shall be included in the annual report required by section one hundred ninety-six of this article.

§ 180. Administrator of the fund

The state comptroller shall appoint and supervise an administrator of the fund. The administrator shall be the chief executive of the fund and shall have the following powers and duties:

1. To represent the state in meetings with the alleged discharger and claimants concerning liability for the discharge and amount of the claims;

2. To determine if hearings are needed to settle particular claims filed by injured persons;

3. To convene hearings;

4. To certify the amount of claims and names of claimants to the state comptroller;

5. To disburse moneys from the fund for cleanup and removal costs pursuant to a certification of claims by the commissioner.

§ 181. Liability

1. Any person who has discharged petroleum shall be strictly liable, without regard to fault, for all cleanup and removal costs and all direct and indirect damages, no matter by whom sustained, as defined in this section. In addition to cleanup and removal costs and damages,

any such person who is notified of such release and who did not undertake relocation of persons residing in the area of the discharge in accordance with paragraph (c) of subdivision seven of section one hundred seventy-six of this article, shall be liable to the fund for an amount equal to two times the actual and necessary expense incurred by the fund for such relocation pursuant to section one hundred seventy-seven-a of this article.

2. The fund shall be strictly liable, without regard to fault, for all cleanup and removal costs and all direct and indirect damages, no matter by whom sustained, including, but not limited to:

(a) The cost of restoring, repairing, or replacing any real or personal property damaged or destroyed by a discharge, any income lost from the time such property is damaged to the time such property is restored, repaired or replaced, any reduction in value of such property caused by such discharge by comparison with its value prior thereto;

(b) The cost of restoration and replacement, where possible, of any natural resource damaged or destroyed by a discharge;

(c) Loss of income or impairment of earning capacity due to damage to real or personal property, including natural resources destroyed or damaged by a discharge; provided that such loss or impairment exceeds ten percent of the amount which claimant derives, based upon income or business records, exclusive of other sources of income, from activities related to the particular real or personal property or natural resources damaged or destroyed by such discharge during the week, month or year for which the claim is filed;

(d) Loss of tax revenue by the state or local governments for a period of one year due to damage to real or personal property proximately resulting from a discharge;

(e) Interest on loans obtained or other obligations incurred by a claimant for the purpose of ameliorating the adverse effects of a discharge pending the payment of a claim in full as provided by this article.

3.

(a) The owner or operator of a major facility or vessel which has discharged petroleum shall be strictly liable, without regard to fault, subject to the defenses enumerated in subdivision four of this section, for all cleanup and removal costs and all direct and indirect damages paid by the fund. However, the cleanup and removal costs and direct and indirect damages which may be recovered by the fund with respect to each incident shall not exceed:

(i) for a tank vessel, the greater of:

(1) one thousand two hundred dollars per gross ton; or

(2)

(A) in the case of a vessel greater than three thousand gross tons, ten million dollars; or

(B) in the case of a vessel or [of]* three thousand gross tons or less, two million dollars;

(ii) for any other vessel subject to the liability limits set forth in the Federal Oil Pollution Act of 1990 (33 U.S.C. 2701 et seq.), six hundred dollars per gross ton or five hundred thousand dollars, whichever is greater;

(iii) for any other vessel not subject to the liability limits set forth in the Federal Oil Pollution Act of 1990 (33 U.S.C. 2701 et seq.), three hundred dollars per gross ton for each vessel;

(iv) for a major facility that is defined as an "onshore facility" and covered by the liability limits established under the Federal Oil Pollution Act of 1990 (33 U.S.C. 2701 et seq.), three hundred fifty million dollars. This liability limit shall not be considered to increase the liability above the federal limit of three hundred fifty million dollars per incident.[;]**

(v) for a major facility not covered in subparagraph (iv) of this paragraph, fifty million dollars.

(b) The liability limits established in subparagraphs (i) and (ii) of paragraph (a) of this subdivision shall not be considered to increase liability above the federal limits for tank vessels or vessels as defined in the Federal Oil Pollution Act of 1990 (33 U.S.C. 2701 et seq.).

(c)

(i) The department shall establish, by regulation, a limit of liability under this subdivision of less than three hundred fifty million dollars but not less than eight million dollars, for major facilities defined as "onshore facilities" under the Federal Oil Pollution Act of 1990 (33 U.S.C. 2701 et seq.), taking into account facility size, storage capacity, throughput, proximity to environmentally sensitive areas, type of petroleum handled, and other factors relevant to risks posed by the class or category of facility.

(ii) The department shall establish, by regulation, a limit of liability under this subdivision of fifty million dollars or less for major facilities other than vessels that are not defined as "onshore facilities" under the Federal Oil Pollution Act of 1990 (33 U.S.C. 2701 et seq.), taking into account facility size, storage capacity, throughput, proximity to environmentally sensitive areas, type of petroleum handled, and other factors relevant to risks posed by the class or category of facility.

(d) The provisions of paragraph (a) of this subdivision shall not apply and the owner or operator shall be liable for the full amount of cleanup and removal costs and damages if it can be shown that the discharge was the result of (i) gross negligence or willful misconduct, within the knowledge and privity of the owner, operator or person in charge, or (ii) a gross or willful violation of applicable safety, construction or operating standards or regulations. In addition, the provisions of paragraph (a) of this subdivision shall not apply if the owner or operator fails or refuses:

(1) to report the discharge as required by section one hundred seventy-five of this article and the owner or operator knows or had reason to know of the discharge; or

(2) to provide all reasonable cooperation and assistance requested by the federal on-scene coordinator or the commissioner or his designee in connection with cleanup and removal activities.

(e)

(i) The owner or operator of a vessel shall establish and maintain with the department evidence of financial responsibility sufficient to meet the amount of liability established pursuant to paragraph (a) of this subdivision. The owner or operator of any vessel which demonstrates financial responsibility pursuant to the requirements of the Federal Oil Pollution Act of 1990 (33 U.S.C. 2701 et seq.), shall be deemed to have demonstrated financial responsibility in accordance with this paragraph.

(ii) The commissioner in consultation with the superintendent of financial services may promulgate regulations requiring the owner or operator of a major facility other than a vessel to establish and maintain evidence of financial responsibility in an amount not to exceed twenty-five dollars, per incident, for each barrel of total petroleum storage capacity at the facility, subject to a maximum of one million dollars per incident per facility in an aggregate not to exceed two million dollars per facility per year; provided, however, that if the owner or operator establishes to the satisfaction of the commissioner that a lesser amount will be sufficient to protect the environment and public health, safety and welfare, the commissioner shall accept evidence of financial responsibility in such lesser amount. In determining the sufficiency of the amount of financial responsibility required under this section, the commissioner and the superintendent of financial services shall take into consideration facility size, storage capacity, throughput, proximity to environmentally sensitive areas, type of petroleum handled, and other factors relevant to the risks posed by the class or category of facility, as well as the availability and affordability of pollution liability insurance. Any regulations promulgated pursuant to this subparagraph shall not take effect until forty-eight months after the effective date of this section.

(iii) Financial responsibility under this paragraph may be established by any one or a combination of the following methods acceptable to the commissioner in consultation with the superintendent of financial services: evidence of insurance, surety bonds, guarantee, letter of credit, qualification as a self-insurer, or other evidence of financial responsibility, including certifications which qualify under the Federal Oil Pollution Act of 1990 (33 U.S.C. 2701 et seq.).

(iv) The liability of a third-party insurer providing proof of financial responsibility on behalf of a person required to establish and maintain evidence of financial responsibility under this section is limited to the type of risk assumed and the amount of coverage specified in the proof of financial responsibility furnished to and approved by the department. For the purposes of this section, the term "third-party insurer" means a third-party insurer, surety, guarantor, person furnishing a letter of credit, or other group or person providing proof of financial responsibility on behalf of another person; it does not include the person required to establish and maintain evidence of such financial responsibility.

4.

(a) The only defenses that may be raised by a person responsible for a discharge of petroleum are: an act or omission caused solely by (i) war, sabotage, or governmental negligence or (ii) an act or omission of a third party other than an employee or agent of the person responsible, or a third party whose act or omission occurs in connection with a contractual relationship with the person responsible, if the person responsible establishes by a preponderance of the evidence that the person responsible (a) exercised due care with respect to the petroleum concerned, taking into consideration the characteristics of petroleum and in light of all relevant facts and circumstances; and (b) took precautions against the acts or omissions of any such third party and the consequences of those acts or omissions. These defenses shall not apply to a person responsible who refuses or fails to (a) report the discharge, or (b) provide all reasonable cooperation and assistance in cleanup and removal activities undertaken on behalf of the fund by the department. In any case where a person responsible for a discharge establishes by a preponderance of the evidence that a discharge and the resulting cleanup and removal costs were caused solely by an act or omission of one or more third parties as described above, the third party or parties shall be treated as the person or persons responsible for the purposes of determining liability under this article.

(b)   Nothing set forth in this subdivision shall be construed to hold a lender liable to the state as a person responsible for the discharge of petroleum at a site in the event: (i) such lender, without participating in the management of such site, holds indicia of ownership primarily to protect the lender's security interest in the site, or (ii) such lender did not participate in the management of such site prior to a foreclosure, and such lender:

(1)   forecloses on such site; and

(2)   after foreclosure, sells, re-leases (in the case of a lease finance transaction), or liquidates such site, maintains business activities, winds up operations, or takes any other measure to preserve, protect or prepare such site for sale or disposition; provided however, that such lender shall take actions to sell, re-lease (in the case of a lease finance transaction), or otherwise divest itself of such site at the earliest practicable, commercially reasonable time, on commercially reasonable terms, taking into account market conditions and legal and regulatory requirements.

(c)   This exemption shall not apply to any lender that has (i) caused or contributed to the discharge of petroleum from or at the site, (ii) purchased, sold, refined, transported, or discharged petroleum from or at such site, or (iii) caused the purchase, sale, refinement, transportation, or discharge of petroleum from or at such site.

The terms "participating in management," "foreclosure," "lender" and "security interest" shall have the same meaning as those terms are defined in paragraph (c) of subdivision one of section 27-1323 of the environmental conservation law.

5. Any claim by any injured person for the costs of cleanup and removal and direct and indirect damages based on the strict liability imposed by this section may be brought directly against the person who has discharged the petroleum, provided, however, that damages recoverable by any injured person in such a direct claim based on the strict liability imposed by this section shall be limited to the damages authorized by this section.

6. Notwithstanding any other provision of this section, a volunteer firefighter, volunteer fire company, volunteer fire district, volunteer fire protection district, or volunteer fire department shall not be strictly liable for discharged petroleum when such discharge results from such volunteer firefighter, volunteer fire company, volunteer fire district, volunteer fire protection district, or volunteer fire department performing his, her, or their firefighting duties and there is not a showing of willful or gross negligence. This subdivision shall not be construed to provide an exemption from liability for a discharge of petroleum on or from real or personal property owned, leased, or operated by any such volunteer fire company, volunteer fire district, volunteer fire protection district, or volunteer fire department.

§ 181-a. Environmental lien

1. The fund shall have a lien for the costs incurred by the fund for the cleanup and removal of a discharge and for the payment of claims for direct and indirect damages as a result of a discharge upon such real property located within the state:

(a) owned by a person liable to the fund for such costs under section one hundred eighty-one of this part at the time a notice of environmental lien is filed; and

(b) upon which the discharge occurred.

2. An environmental lien shall attach when:

(a) cleanup and removal costs and damage costs are incurred by the fund;

(b) the person referred to in subdivision one of this section fails to pay such costs within ninety days after a written demand therefor by the administrator is mailed by certified or registered mail, return receipt requested; and

(c) a notice of environmental lien is filed as provided in section one hundred eighty-one-c of this part; provided, however, that a copy of the notice of environmental lien is served upon the owner of the real property subject to the environmental lien within thirty days of such filing in accordance with the provisions of section eleven of the lien law.

3. An environmental lien shall continue against the real property until:

(a) the claim or judgment against the person referred to in subdivision one of this section for cleanup and removal costs and damage costs is satisfied or becomes unenforceable;

(b) the lien is released by the administrator pursuant to this subdivision;

(c) the lien is discharged by payment of moneys into court; or

(d) the lien is otherwise vacated by court order.

Upon the occurrence of any of the foregoing, except where the lien is vacated by court order, the administrator shall execute the release of an environmental lien and file the release as provided in section one hundred eighty-one-c of this part. The administrator may release an environmental lien where:

(i) a legally enforceable agreement satisfactory to the administrator has been executed relating to cleanup and removal costs and damage costs or reimbursing the fund for cleanup and removal costs and damage costs; or

(ii) the attachment or enforcement of the environmental lien is determined by the administrator not to be in the public interest.

4. An environmental lien is subject to the rights of any other person, including an owner, purchaser, holder of a mortgage or security interest, or judgment lien creditor, whose interest is perfected before a lien notice has been filed as provided in section one hundred eighty-one-c of this part.

§ 181-b. Environmental lien notice; contents

A notice of environmental lien must state:

1. That the lienor is the New York environmental protection and spill compensation fund;

2. The name of the record owner of the real property on which the environmental lien has attached;

3. The real property subject to the lien, with a description thereof sufficient for identification;

4. That the real property described in the notice is the property upon which a discharge occurred and that cleanup and removal costs and damage costs have been incurred by the lienor as a result of such discharge;

5. That the owner is potentially liable for cleanup and removal costs and damage costs

pursuant to section one hundred eighty-one of this part; and

6. That an environmental lien has attached to the described real property.

§ 181-c. Filing of notice of environmental lien; filing of release

1. A notice of environmental lien shall be filed within six years from the time a disbursement is made by the fund for cleanup and removal costs and damage costs incurred by the fund in the clerk's office of the county where the property is situated. If such property is situated in two or more counties, the notice of environmental lien shall be filed in the office of the clerk of each of such counties. The notice of lien shall be indexed by the county clerk in accordance with the provisions of section ten of the lien law.

2. A release of an environmental lien shall be filed in the clerk's office of each county where the notice of environmental lien was filed and shall be indexed in the manner prescribed for indexing environmental liens.

§ 181-d. Enforcement of environmental lien

An environmental lien may be enforced against the property specified in the notice of environmental lien, and an environmental lien may be vacated or discharged, as prescribed in article three of the lien law; provided, however, that nothing in this article or in article three of the lien law shall affect the right of the fund to bring an action to recover cleanup and removal costs and damage costs under section one hundred eighty-one, one hundred eighty-seven, one hundred eighty-eight or one hundred ninety of this part.

§ 181-e. Amounts received to satisfy lien

Amounts received by the administrator to satisfy all or part of an environmental lien shall be deposited in the state treasury and credited to the environmental protection and spill compensation fund.

§ 182. Claims against the fund

Claims shall be filed with the administrator not later than three years after the date of discovery of damage nor later than ten years after the date of the incident which caused the damage. The administrator shall prescribe appropriate forms and procedures for such claims, which shall include a provision requiring the claimant to make a sworn verification of the claim to the best of his knowledge. Any person who knowingly gives or causes to be given any false information as a part of any such claim shall, in addition to any other penalties herein or elsewhere prescribed, be guilty of a misdemeanor punishable by a fine of up to one thousand dollars or up to one year imprisonment. Upon receipt of any claim, the administrator shall as soon as practicable inform all affected parties of the claim.

§ 183. Settlements

The administrator shall attempt to promote and arrange a settlement between the claimant and the person responsible for the discharge. If the source of the discharge can be determined and liability is conceded, the claimant and the alleged discharger may agree to a settlement which shall be final and binding upon the parties and which will waive all recourse against the fund.

§ 184. Settlements when source of discharge is unknown

If the source of the discharge is unknown or cannot be determined, the claimant and the administrator shall attempt to arrange a settlement of any claim against the fund. The administrator is authorized to enter and certify payment of such settlement subject to such proof and procedures contained in regulations promulgated by the administrator.

§ 185. Hearings for persons on claims filed with the administrator

1. The administrator shall grant a hearing when persons alleged to be responsible for the discharge contest the validity or amount of damage claims or claims for cleanup and removal costs presented by injured persons to the fund for payment or when injured persons who have filed a claim against the fund contest the validity or amount of the settlement proposed by the administrator.

2. One hearing may be granted to hear and determine all claims arising from or related to a common discharge.

3. The burden of proof with respect to the validity or amount of damage claims or claims for cleanup and removal costs shall be upon the persons contesting such claims or the claimants contesting the settlement proposed by the administrator.

4. At least twenty days notice of such hearing shall be given by the administrator to the claimants and, if known, the alleged dischargers.

5. Upon the return day of such notice the person so notified shall file with the administrator a statement setting forth the position of the person so notified. Pertinent and relevant testimony of witnesses shall be received in support of or opposition to said statement. The

claimants or alleged dischargers may appear in person or by attorney, present witnesses, submit evidence and be given full opportunity to be heard.

6. The administrator shall have the power to order testimony under oath and may subpoena attendance and testimony of witnesses and the production of such documentary materials pertinent to the issues presented at the hearing. Each person appearing at the hearing may be represented by counsel.

7. Within sixty calendar days from the close of such hearing and after due consideration of the written and oral statements and testimony and arguments filed pursuant to this section, or on default in appearance on said return day, the administrator shall make a final determination on the validity or amount of the damage claims or claims for cleanup and removal costs filed by the injured persons. The administrator shall notify the claimant and, if known, the alleged discharger thereof in writing by registered mail.

8. Determinations made by the administrator after such hearing shall be final and conclusive. Any action for judicial review shall be filed pursuant to the provisions of article seventy-eight of the civil practice law and rules.

9. Upon a determination by the administrator that provides for an award to the claimants, the administrator shall certify the amount of the award and the name of the claimant to the state comptroller, who shall pay the award from the fund. In any case in which a person responsible for the discharge seeks judicial review, reasonable attorney's fees and costs shall be awarded to the claimant if the determination of the administrator is affirmed.

§ 186. Disbursement of moneys from the fund

1.

(a) Moneys in the account established by paragraph (a) of subdivision two of section one hundred seventy-nine of this part shall be disbursed by the administrator, upon certification by the commissioner, for the purpose of costs incurred under section one hundred seventy-six of this article. (i) Beginning in state fiscal year two thousand fifteen—two thousand sixteen, up to two million one hundred thousand dollars per year shall be appropriated to the department for use only for the oil spill prevention and training purposes authorized in subdivision three of this section.

(b) Moneys in the account established by paragraph (b) of subdivision two of section one hundred seventy-nine of this part shall, within forty-five days of the close of each license fee period, be deposited by the administrator, in the hazardous waste remedial fund created pursuant to section ninety-seven-b of the state finance law for expenditure pursuant to such section; provided, however, that the state comptroller shall cause the administrator to reimburse the commissioner for the reasonable costs of collecting the surcharge during those times when the license fee is not imposed.

2. Moneys in the account established by paragraph (a) of subdivision two of section one hundred seventy-nine of this part shall be disbursed by the administrator, upon certification by him, for the following purposes:

(a) Damages as defined in section one hundred eighty-one of this article;

(b) Such sums as may be necessary for research on the prevention and the effects of spills of petroleum on the environment and on the development of improved cleanup and removal operations as may be appropriated by the legislature; provided, however, that such sums shall not exceed the amount of interest which is credited to the account established by paragraph (a) of subdivision two of section one hundred seventy-nine of this part;

(c) Such sums as may be necessary for the general administration of the fund, equipment and personnel costs of the department of environmental conservation and any other state agency related to the enforcement of this article as may be appropriated by the legislature;

(d) Such sums as may be appropriated by the legislature for research and demonstration programs concerning the causes and abatement of ocean pollution; provided, however, that such sums shall not exceed the amount of interest which is credited to the account established by paragraph (a) of subdivision two of section one hundred seventy-nine of this part.

(e) Such sums as may be necessary for the general administration, equipment and personnel costs of the department of environmental conservation related to the administration and enforcement of the petroleum bulk storage program established pursuant to title ten of article seventeen of the environmental conservation law.

3. Moneys appropriated to the department pursuant to subparagraph (i) of paragraph (a) of subdivision one of this section, up to two million one hundred thousand dollars, shall be disbursed only for the following purposes:

(a) Such sums as may be necessary for the acquisition and maintenance of petroleum spill prevention, response or personal safety equipment and supplies and training for state and local government entities, including emergency services agencies and personnel.

(b) Such sums as may be necessary for petroleum spill response drills and exercises.

(c) Such sums as may be necessary for identification, mapping, and analysis of populations, environmentally sensitive areas, and resources at risk from spills of petroleum and related impacts; and the development, implementation, and updating of contingency plans, including geographic response plans, to protect those populations, sensitive environments, and resources in the event of a spill of petroleum or related impacts.

(d) Spending pursuant to this subdivision shall be included in the annual report required by section one hundred ninety-six of this article.

4. Moneys shall be disbursed from the fund only for the purposes set forth in subdivisions one, two and three of this section.

5. The state comptroller may invest and reinvest any moneys in said fund in obligations in which the comptroller is authorized to invest pursuant to the provisions of section ninety-eight-a of the state finance law. Any income or interest derived from such investment shall be included in the fund.

§ 187. Reimbursements of moneys to fund

The administrator shall recover to the fund moneys disbursed for the following purposes:

1. Costs incurred by the fund in the cleanup and removal of a discharge when the person responsible for causing a discharge has failed to promptly clean up and remove the discharge to the satisfaction of the department;

2. Costs incurred by the fund in the payment of claims for direct and indirect damages, as defined in section one hundred eighty-one of this article; and

3. All penalties assessed pursuant to this article.

§ 188. Subrogation of rights

Payment of any cleanup costs or damages by the fund arising from a single incident shall be conditioned upon the administrator acquiring by subrogation all rights of the claimant to recovery of such costs or damages from the discharger or other responsible party. The administrator shall then seek satisfaction from the discharger or other responsible party in the supreme court if the discharger or other responsible party does not reimburse the fund. In any such suit, except as provided by section one hundred eighty-one of this article, the administrator need prove only that an unlawful discharge occurred which was the responsibility of the discharger or other responsible party. The administrator is hereby authorized and empowered to compromise and settle the amount sought for cost and damages from the discharger or other responsible party and any penalty arising under this article.

§ 189. Awards exceeding current balance

In the event that the total awards for a specific occurrence exceed the current balance of the fund, the immediate award shall be paid on a prorated basis, and all claimants paid on a prorated basis shall be paid as determined by the administrator, a pro rata share of all moneys received by the fund until the total amount of the proven damages is paid to the claimant or claimants. The administrator may also provide through regulation to fix the priority for the payment of claims based on extreme hardship.

§ 190. Claims against insurers

Any claims for costs of cleanup and removal, civil penalties or damages by the state and any claim for damages by any injured person, may be brought directly against the bond, the insurer, or any other person providing evidence of financial responsibility.

§ 190-a. Application of article

For purposes of cleanup and removal of any public or private ground water supply system contaminated by a discharge occurring either before or after the effective date of article twelve of this chapter, all relevant provisions of article twelve of this chapter shall apply.

Part FOUR Miscellaneous

§ 191. Joint rules and regulations

The commissioner and the state comptroller are authorized to adopt, amend, repeal, and enforce such rules and regulations pursuant to the state administrative procedure act, as they may deem necessary to accomplish the purposes of this article.

§ 192. Enforcement of article; penalties

Any person who knowingly gives or causes to be given any false information as a part of, or in response to, any claim made pursuant to this article for cleanup and removal costs, direct or indirect damages resulting from a discharge, or who otherwise violates any of the provisions of this article or any rule promulgated thereunder or who fails to comply with any duty created by this article shall be liable to a penalty of not more than twenty-five thousand dollars for each offense in a court of competent jurisdiction. If the violation is of a continuing nature each day during which it continues shall constitute an additional, separate and distinct offense.

§ 193. Availability of additional remedies

Nothing in this article shall be deemed to preclude the pursuit of any other civil or injunctive remedy by any person. The remedies provided in this article are in addition to those provided by existing statutory or common law, but no person who receives compensation for damages or cleanup and removal costs pursuant to any other state or federal law shall be permitted to receive compensation for the same damages or cleanup and removal costs under this article.

§ 194. Severability

If any section, subdivision, provision, clause or portion of this article is adjudged unconstitutional or invalid by a court of competent jurisdiction, the remainder of this article shall not be affected thereby.

§ 195. Construction

This article, being necessary for the general health, safety, and welfare of the people of this state, shall be liberally construed to effect its purposes.

§ 196. Reports

The commissioner and the administrator shall make an annual report to the legislature and the governor which shall describe the quality and quantity of spills of petroleum, the costs and damages paid by and recovered for the fund, and moneys spent pursuant to subdivision three of section one hundred eighty-six of this article including amounts spent for oil spill prevention and training activities conducted, and equipment purchased, and the economic and environmental impact on the state as a result of the administration of this article.

§ 197. Effect of federal legislation

If the United States congress enacts legislation providing compensation in the event of a discharge of petroleum, the commissioner shall determine to what degree that legislation provides the needed protection for our citizens, businesses and environment and shall make the appropriate recommendations to the legislature for amendments to this article.

Article 13 Miscellaneous Provisions; Saving Clause; Laws Repealed; When to Take Effect

§ 200. Collection of penalties

1. An action to recover any penalty imposed under the provisions of this chapter, except penalties imposed under article six, may be brought in any court of competent jurisdiction in this state on order of the commissioner and in the name of the people of the state of New York. In any such action all penalties incurred up to the time of commencing the action may be sued for and recovered therein and the commencement of an action to recover any such penalty shall not be, or be held to be, a waiver of the right to recover any other penalty. In case of recovery of any amount in an action brought to recover any such penalty the people shall be entitled to recover full costs, of course, and at the rates provided for civil actions.

2. Judgments recovered may be enforced by contempt. A person taken into custody shall be confined for not less than one day, and at the rate of one day for each dollar of the amount of the judgment recovered. No person shall be imprisoned more than once, or for more than six months on the same judgment. Imprisonment shall not operate to satisfy a judgment.

3. No person shall be excused from testifying or producing any books, papers or other documents in any civil action to recover any such penalty, upon the ground that his testimony might tend to convict him of a crime, or to subject him to a penalty or forfeiture. But no person shall be prosecuted, punished, or subjected to any penalty or forfeiture for or on account of any act, transaction, matter or thing concerning which he shall, under oath, have testified or produced documentary evidence and no testimony so given or produced shall be received against him upon any criminal investigation or proceeding; provided, however, that no person so testifying shall be exempt from prosecution or punishment for any perjury committed by him in his testimony. Nothing herein contained is intended to give, or shall be construed as in any manner giving, unto any corporation, immunity of any kind.

4. A person who has violated any of such provisions and who desires to compromise and settle his civil liability therefor may appear with the inspector before a court or justice having jurisdiction in civil actions, and thereupon such person may upon consent of the inspector, compromise and settle his liability for such civil penalties for an amount agreed upon between said court or justice, the inspector and the person who committed such violation, which amount shall be not less than ten dollars nor more than the amount for which such person would be liable in a civil action for penalties. If such compromise be made, such person shall forthwith subscribe his name to a statement setting forth concisely the facts constituting such violation, the amount agreed upon, and that a judgment may be entered against him for that sum. Upon said statement being sworn to before and filed with said court or justice, he shall forthwith enter in his civil docket a record of the proceedings and the amount of the judgment. Said court or justice shall upon the entry of said judgment be entitled to a fee of two dollars and fifty cents to be paid by the person who committed such violation. A judgment entered into pursuant to this subdivision may be enforced by an execution against the property of the defendant; but no body execution shall be issued thereon.

5. The court or justice before whom any person shall be tried or before whom a compromise of the civil penalties shall have been made, or the clerk of the court, if there be a clerk, shall at the termination of such trial or proceeding, forthwith mail or deliver to the department at Albany, a certified statement of the disposition of the case or proceeding, giving the date thereof, the name of the defendant, the date and place of the violation, the name of each witness sworn in support of the charges and the costs of the court or fees of the justice, the fees of the constable or other peace officer, police officer or traveling navigation inspector, if any, together with the amount of the penalty paid.

6. The provisions of this section shall in no way prohibit the prosecution of violations of this chapter in any court of competent jurisdiction in the same manner as other offenses and crimes.

§ 201. Disposition of fees and penalties

1. On the first day of each month or within ten days thereafter, all fines and penalties collected for violations of this chapter, except for violations of article six, under judgment of

any town or village court or justice or pursuant to compromise, shall be paid over by such court or justice to the comptroller of the state, with a statement accompanying the same, setting forth the action or proceeding in which such moneys were collected, the name and residence of the defendant, the nature of the offense, and the fine or penalty imposed.

2. All fines and penalties, except for violations of article six of this chapter, collected for violations of this chapter by courts operating pursuant to section thirty-nine of the judiciary law shall be paid to the state commissioner of taxation and finance on a monthly basis no later than ten days after the last day of each month.

3. All fines and penalties imposed for violations of article four of this chapter under judgment of any town or village court or justice or pursuant to compromise which are paid over by such court or justice to the comptroller shall be deposited by the comptroller into the "I love NY waterways" boating safety fund established pursuant to section ninety-seven-nn of the state finance law.

§ 202. Application and saving clause

Any work or proceeding initiated under any existing law which is repealed through the enactment of this chapter shall be continued legally to its termination and conclusion subject to the provisions of and in accordance with the procedure prescribed by such law. It is the intent that upon the enactment of this chapter into law all proceedings undertaken thereafter relative to the navigable waters of the state, as defined in this chapter, shall be administered under the authority of and by the provisions contained in this chapter. Upon all waters where the United States authorities have established active control of navigation, any part of this chapter which is contrary to or in conflict with the United States navigation law, or with regulations issued pursuant thereto, shall be considered inoperative and the pertinent part of the United States law or regulation shall apply. It is the intent upon enactment of this chapter that no provision hereof shall affect or impair in any manner whatsoever any provision of chapter two hundred eighty-five of the laws of nineteen hundred forty. If any clause, sentence, paragraph or part of this chapter shall, for any reason be adjudged by any court of competent jurisdiction to be invalid, such judgment shall not affect, impair or invalidate the remainder thereof but shall be confined in its operation to the clause, sentence, paragraph or part thereof, directly involved in the controversy in which such judgment shall have been rendered. Nothing contained in this chapter shall be construed to abridge the terms of office of the board of commissioners of pilots in the city of New York; nor to limit or restrict the powers of such board under article six, nor to confer a power or impose a duty upon the commissioner relating thereto.

§ 203. Laws repealed

Chapter forty-two of the laws of nineteen hundred nine, entitled "An act relating to navigation, constituting chapter thirty-seven of the consolidated laws," and chapter two hundred and ninety-two of the laws of nineteen hundred forty, entitled "An act relating to navigation on and use of the waters of Lake Placid" and all acts and parts of acts amendatory of or supplemental to any of such chapters or sections and all acts or parts of acts inconsistent with the provisions of this chapter are hereby repealed. The repeal of chapter forty-two of the laws of nineteen hundred nine as amended, and chapter two hundred and ninety-two of the laws of nineteen hundred forty shall not operate or be construed to terminate any license heretofore issued thereunder or affect the rights of any person holding such a license; nor shall such repeal affect any action or proceeding now pending in any court, or any act done or right accruing, accrued or acquired, or penalty, forfeiture or punishment inflicted pursuant to such chapters, or either of them, prior to the date this act takes effect; but the same may be asserted, enforced, prosecuted or inflicted as fully and to the same extent as if this act had not been passed, or such chapters had not been repealed.

§ 204. When to take effect

This act shall take effect July first, nineteen hundred forty-one, except section seventy-one thereof, which section shall take effect January first, nineteen hundred forty-two.

www.ingramcontent.com/pod-product-compliance
Lightning Source LLC
Chambersburg PA
CBHW080959170526
45158CB00010B/2841